OPENING A PET GROOMING SALON

10 Steps to Success

Tanya Ellis

OPENING A PET GROOMING SALON: 10 Steps to Success

www.poochesandpalsinc.com

Publisher: Columbus Book Publishers

www.columbusbookpublishers.com

Printed in the United States of America

This book is dedicated to the young ones in my life, whom are all at different stages of their life but inspire me: Mariah, Madison, Hannah, Jonah, Koah, and Tamiyah.
Love you all beyond words, and want the very best for you in your future. Remember, you can accomplish anything you put your mind to.

Testimonials

Tanya and her team are the best groomers by a landslide, and I've tried many! Our little dog, Doug, is very finicky with his grooming, and after bringing him to Pooches N' Pals, he always comes home happy, well-groomed, and oh-so-professional looking! I am so happy to have found such trustworthy and caring people! Would recommend to friends and family without a second thought!
– Emma Wallace, with Doug

Pooches N' Pals has been taking care of my fur baby for over two years now. They are awesome, with amazing staff. Tanya is a great groomer and has helped us understand the needs and expectations for Luke. They always take good care of him and make him super comfortable.
– Jai Kohli, with Luke

I have had my Goldendoodle, Simba, groomed at Pooches N' Pals four times now, and I am completely satisfied. Tanya and her team are absolutely wonderful. They are extremely kind, professional, caring, patient, and, above all, talented at what they do. I couldn't imagine taking Simba anywhere else. In fact, I drive from northeast Brampton all the way to Port Credit just to have him groomed there. I highly recommend Pooches N' Pals, you won't find better groomers.
– Gregory Danakas, with Simba

Tanya and her team are the best of the best! My dog has been going there for almost eight years now, and he always gets so excited (a really good indicator of how well they care for the dogs they groom). They always listen to your concerns and ensure that they give you exactly what you're looking for! There are plenty of grooming options, and your preferences are always noted. Thank you so much, Tanya and team; you always make my dog's day!!!
– Aoife Brereton, with Roman

What a great experience! We have a very fluffy, almost one-year-old Goldendoodle, which we didn't want shaved to the skin. We took him to a couple of groomers, and all they wanted to do was shave him right to the skin (assuming it's the easiest option?). His hair is changing to adult hair, so he was a little matted despite me brushing him every day. Pooches N' Pals' professional groomers were able to do a great job without shaving him completely! They called me a few times to confirm if it was okay to shave him shorter than what we had discussed in certain areas where he was matted. We will definitely go back!
– Mona, with Freddy

Acknowledgements

I would like to acknowledge the author, Rhonda Byrne for writing the book *The Secret* and for inspiring me when times were not so great in my life. If it weren't for all the amazing information in this book, a lot of the struggles that happened when I was young would have felt more like mountains I had to climb. So, from the bottom of my heart, I thank you so much for your inspiring words and for making me believe in myself.

I would like to acknowledge Raymond Aaron for his incredible knowledge on how to write a book in a short period of time. His knowledge and expertise in this field are second to none. I am so humbled that I had the opportunity to take his three-day "Get Your Book Done" course. Thank you, Raymond Aaron Team, for helping to change my life for the better.

If I had the opportunity to thank every single one of my clients by name, this would take up the entire book. My long-time love for all the clients of Pooches N' Pals cannot be expressed. Your pooches made me so happy every day when I got to go in and make them look their best, day after day. Because I can't fit everyone's name inside this acknowledgement section, I am going to take a moment and personally thank each and every one of you for giving me the opportunity to care for your pets!

Another book that inspired me was by Melissa Verplank. Her book, *Notes From the Grooming Table*, has helped me in my business. Thanks to your book, I have been able to inspire many other groomers to read it and follow directions on how to properly groom a dog. Thank you so much, Melissa!

I would like to take the opportunity to thank Tony Robbins. Because of the Business Mastery program that I just took, I'm finally getting something off my bucket list by writing this book. My heart is so overwhelmed with joy from the knowledge and energy you provide. I cannot be more grateful than I am right now!

To my husband, Anthony Ierullo, no words can actually express how grateful I am to have you in my life! You are one of a kind, you are my rock, you are my love, you are my everything. I owe you so much. Because of you, I am stronger, more disciplined, and more motivated! You helped me figure out what I didn't believe was possible. I honestly can't thank you enough for everything that you've done for me all these years. We are just two peas in a pod, and I love you more and more every day! Thank you for being my "everything!"

To my mom (Elke Proulx), you've been there for everything. You're my mom, but you also helped build Pooches N' Pals for the past eight years, and I'm forever grateful to you. Mom, you are always there when I need to talk about something, and you are so understanding of me. You are also the sweetest, kindest mom. I love you to the moon and back. XO

To my dad (Alain Proulx), you've always been there to test my knowledge on subjects that I really had no idea about, but I pretended to, and we would debate. This made me have more freedom of speech and not worry about what other people think.

It also taught me to have an open mind, which is extremely important in this day and age! Not to mention all the times you and Mom took us (our family) on vacations, brought me lunches, drove me everywhere, and were just there for me. I'm forever grateful to both of you, and I wouldn't be the person I am today if it weren't for you! I love you so much. XO

To my sister, Leah Duval, my complete opposite. Even though I'm older than you, you were always the one I looked up to! You taught me so much about how to be confident, how to have style, and how to fit in. You had the strength that I always wished I had! Growing up, we went through a lot; we had our fair share of arguments (that's an understatement), but in the end, we have always been there for one another! I watch you with your son (my nephew) Koah, and I am so proud of the mother you have become! I love you so much! Let's always keep the past behind us! XO

To Marc, Hannah, and Jonah Duval, thank you for being part of Leah's life and part of her happiness. We are thrilled to have you as part of our family. Love you all very much.

To my kid sister, Tiffany Proulx (Kidd), you will always be my kid sister. We've always been close no matter what, with just a few bumps in the road! I love you so much. Your sense of humor is something that no one else I know has, other than Dad of course. It's always been a quality that I've admired about you! You always help people see the light in situations! I'm so happy that I'm an auntie again. Tamiyah is beautiful, and I can't wait to do all the fun things together. Love you, kiddo; keep smiling. XO

To Taymaa, for being there for Tiffany; you are one of the sweetest, most caring people I know, and she is so lucky to have you. I am so proud that you are my brother-in-law. Your family are also some of the most caring people I know.

To Madison Ierullo and Mariah Ierullo, you two girls are so special and sweet. Thank you for being part of the reason that I wanted to make this happen. Keep reaching for the stars and going after your dreams, and don't let anybody stop you! XO

Steve Ballantyne, our neighbor and friend, whom I have looked up to for many years, you have been there to chat and run ideas off of and have helped me understand your view on business, and it has been really refreshing to be able to talk to you. I also appreciate you holding me accountable and helping me edit this book. Thank you so much for your kindness, honesty, and advice.

I want to acknowledge my team from Pooches N' Pals, past and present. If it weren't for them, I wouldn't be where I am today! This team is so incredible; they work their tails off to make sure that dogs are cared for in the same way that I would! To my team, you amaze me and delight me with how motivated and passionate you are. Thank you to my mom (Elke Proulx), Monika Kubik, Sylvie Tremblay, Melisa Singh, Melissa Black, Samantha Paulino, Allison Durrell, Nick Brooks, Izabella Soares, and Alicia Pellizzoni.

The members of the Worldwide Pet Grooming Association: You all were there when no one else was. You were shoulders to lean on and cry on when our industry was going through a tough time during the pandemic. Each one of you inspired me to be a better person, and for that, I am so grateful. I hope that I gave you inspiration in a time when there really wasn't any. Lindsay Buccella, Lucy Loren, Colleen Zuber, Stephanie Louise Bajona, Nova Wesley-Yausie, Steph Petro, Brenda Bott, Brianna Vincent, Melissa Jill Snider, Jenny Ellen Oliver, Becky Burgoyne, Genny

Mount, Donna Doucette, Crystal Allard, Kristin Berry-Fagundes, Sara Cameron, Karen Leggat, Shara Fancey, Alyssa Tower, Alessandra Bicknell, Anchalee Theeraptporn, Deaana McGuire, Valerie June Carte, and Anna Carte, you will always have a special place in my heart. Love, Tanya.

Thank you, Brenda Bott; you know what you did. I will take it to the grave and will never forget how humble you are.

My Pug, Sandy, for her unconditional love and her strength. Rest in peace, my baby girl.

My Poodle, Stuey, for always making me laugh and snuggling me when I'm down.

To Sara Bird, for capturing the photo of me in my happy place, at the salon of my dreams. I just love this picture. Thank you, Sara, from Sara Noah Photography.

To Britney Spears, for your music; I just love your tunes.

And Taylor Swift, "Shake It Off" is one of my go-to blast songs in my Jeep when I need to be lifted up and get rid of negative vibes.

To Vanessa De Prophetis, for providing entertaining TikToks that are fun and educational.

To my Opa, who is no longer with us; I feel like I have been inspired by you and your entrepreneurship for my whole life.

To Sherri Davis, the host of *How 2 Dog* and the trainer for Diesel from *Hudson and Rex*, you were the first business owner that I looked up to. I thought you were so important, and I was so inspired by how so many pet parents loved you. I am in awe of your success and continue to follow your accomplishments on social media. Thank you for teaching me about dogs and for the opportunity to have you take a chance on me.

To Stephen Dasko, our Ward 1 Councilor, for giving me hope during the pandemic and hearing out my concerns.

To Bonnie Crombie, for listening to me during the pandemic and getting groomers open in Mississauga first. You took a risk, and many other mayors followed suit. I'm so happy that you took the time to hear me out.

To Rudy Cuzzetto, for taking many emails and calls from me and making sure my voice was heard.

To Dog Tales, for rescuing dogs and making sure your team has an amazing working environment, with a beautiful lunchroom to relax in during downtime. Your cause is incredible, and the work you do there is amazing.

To the Lions Foundation of Canada Dog Guides, for the work you do in providing dog guides to people in need. Your cause is near and dear to my heart, as I really feel that dogs make a huge difference in people's lives.

To Cesar Millan, the "Dog Whisperer," for inspiring me throughout the years and teaching me about energy in dogs and how they respond to our positive energy. I have learned so much from you by watching and learning your techniques.

To my BFFs, Vicky Ross, Andrew Ross, Damon Ross, Kyle Ross, Liam Ross, and Mason Ross, and also Mark and Sheila Golding and

Sue Woods, some of my biggest supporters. You all have always been there for me, and I am truly grateful for your friendship. Love you all so much.

To the Best in Show Dog Grooming students, current and future, Fatima Amaral, Jennifer Carfagnini, and Maria Kirslia. The four of you have helped me grow in a way that you cannot even imagine. Taking me out of my comfort zone and helping me help you learn a passion is very inspiring. You all are doing so well, and I am so proud of your progress.

Thank you, Karen Meeker; your friendship is really important to me. I love our chats and catching up. It's really nice having someone who is there to hear you out.

Thank you, Kelly Best; your friendship is really important to me. I have always admired your smile and confidence.

Thank you, Christine Giampietro, for your friendship all these years and for bringing Milo in to see us at Pooches N' Pals.

Thank you, Willie Dominick, for being a great leader and for giving me one of my first jobs, and teaching me the importance of hard work.

Thank you to the teammates from the Beer Store, who showed me how to be a team player. I developed some amazing friendships over the years and am forever grateful for meeting you all.

Thank you, Steve Elliott, my manager from when I worked at PetSmart. You and I had so many one-on-one meetings, and you helped me through so many problems that I encountered as a new manager. You really helped me realize my potential, and I developed more as a leader because of your assistance.

Thank you, Jen Sincero, for writing the book *You Are a Badass at Making Money*. This book helped me make a few major decisions in the past year and really helped me with my growth. I'm so grateful to you for writing it.

Thank you, Anthony Gallippi, for your continued advice regarding real estate.

Thank you, Oleg Shiller, for your mortgage advice and for making sure we make the right choices financially for our current position.

To any leader who was in my life, and to the ones who were not so nice, especially those who challenged me, it was because of you that I was driven to become the entrepreneur that I am today.

Thank you, April Nickles and Desire Nickles. You were always great friends to me, and I miss you terribly. We seem to never get the chance to hang out, and I miss that. You always believed in me, and I am forever grateful for our friendship.

To Nick Ierullo, Anne Mecca, Franca and Michael Agnes, Pina and David Wunder, Katherine Wunder, Kristina Wunder, Joseph Wunder, Mandy Karnis, Joanna Bennink, Rick Bennink, Lilliana and Paul, Candice, Tanya, Jasmine and Chelsea Sanascartier, and Victor Carito, Alex Mecca, Tyler Mecca, Mike Ierullo and Michelle Ierullo, for being there for me all these years and including me as family (I know I am!). I have felt the love all these years.

To Pauline Magri Pierson, for always being the first one to support all of my new endeavours in business. Kaiser and Wini are so special. XO

To Kathy Armstrong, for your friendship. You are an inspirational woman, and I love you. We were always great friends, and I wish we could see each other more.

To Maria and Vince Pimpinella, for being great friends and making me feel special.

Blair, Diane, Cassie, Adam, and David Munn, for being a family that has been in my life for so long, supporting everything I do. I still feel like we are an extended family, and I love you all very much.

To Lynn Holliday, for teaching me about real estate and helping us buy our first home. I am truly grateful for that, and it was an experience I will never forget.

To my fellow Kilimanjaro team, you know who you are: Debbie Bunze, Dave Albano, Cathy Goodale, Roxanne Gural, Angela, Bruce Elliott, Christeine Gaddey, Jasmine Theberge, Ronald Shane Releeder, Leah Cournoyer, Belinda Lamoca, Kirsty Spence, Jane Haque, Bart Mann, Aaron, Alfie, Ryan Turnbull, Robin, Angela Ong, and Mark Outram. We had an unforgettable experience, and I am forever grateful.

To my team, the Sexy Condors, who inspired me and stayed so positive during our Inca Trail trek in Machu Picchu. It was a pleasure hiking with you, and you are all so special: Eckhardt Horstmann, Louise Dignam, Karl Spark (thank you for carrying my bag during the tough parts), Renee Edwards, Catherine Isted, Jen Bueno, Frankie Bell, Eric Bueno, and Patrick Luu.

To anyone who has ever referred out a small business to another person, your kind words are never forgotten and are always appreciated.

To Julia Chatterji, for your friendship. It's nice to have business owners as friends, to run ideas by once in a while, and just be there for each other.

To Michelle McAuley, for being a great leader and friend through the years.

To Rollande Proulx and Andre Morin, for your support through the years. Love you very much.

To my Tenta Myriam and Uncle Alain, my Tenta Angela and Uncle Louie, my Uncle Johnny and Tenta Lisha Elizabeth De Wilde, and my cousins Yan Lorite, Alida Klein, Nick Klein, John Klein, and Janine Guenette. We had so much fun growing up at Opa's house, and all the get-togethers were so nice. I am so grateful to have all of you in my life.

To the team at Erin Mills Pet Hospital, for always referring us out. I am truly grateful that you think so highly of our grooming team. Your team is amazing and caring, and you also take great care of all of my babies, Willie, Sandy, and Stuey. Thank you so much!

To Sandra McClure and Ren's Pets Depot, for asking us to take part in events with Ren's. It really did help our business grow, and you have always been huge supporters of groomers.

To all of the groomers who inspired me through the years, whom I have learned from and who helped me grow, you know who you are. To name a few: Priscilla Suddard, Ann Curran, Olga Zabelinskaya, Billie Jo Horvath, Joshua Morales, Kat Early, Melanie Crowther, Lisa Leady, Lindsey Dicken, Terri Hotchkiss, Bullet Brown, Katleyn Peterman, Irina Pinkusevich, Philip Schafmayer, Blake Hernandez, Isabella Jane Doblas Jones, Barbara Prueckel, Shauna Bernardin, Wynne Wong, Jackie Boulton, and Paddy Gaffney Heuvelmans.

To my first-ever clients who brought their pets to me in my parents' basement when I first wanted to try becoming an entrepreneur. I never forget that, and it is so near and dear to my heart.

To all the bullies in my life when I was younger: Thinking back now, it wouldn't bother me at all today. I am so grateful that it happened back then because it made me so strong today!

To everyone that said "no" to me, it made me try harder for "yeses."

To some of the teammates that are no longer with me, you are never forgotten and are always appreciated. I thank you for everything you taught me over the years and apologize for any heartache I may have caused you. I remember some times when I was going through stuff, which we all do, right? No excuse, but I did learn from my mistakes, and if I could take back anything that caused anyone hurt, I would. But the past is the past for a reason. I wish you luck in your future endeavors.

To Mika Amitoviski Midolo, for believing in the Worldwide Pet Grooming Association.

To Melissa Hancock, for posting about Stuey. Because of that, I found a perfect dog match for my life.

To Dorota and Gil Lorenson, for letting me bring Paree to grooming shows and placing with him several times. It helped me grow as a groomer. I am so grateful for this.

To Amanda Von Besser, for being a great friend all these years. It's been nice having someone that I can chat with regularly with no judgment. We have been friends forever. Let's keep it up. XO

To Maggie and Sam from Maggie's Diner, we went through so much together during the pandemic, and it was great to have you there to bounce ideas off of and to help each other through that crazy time in 2020 and 2021.

To Peggie Liederman, for taking care of my accounting needs and being someone I could bounce business ideas off of all these years. I am so lucky to have you in my life to talk to, and you are someone I fully trust.

To Beverly McKee, I have admired you as a person and a trainer and for all you do. Thank you for our friendship all these years.

To Carolyn Abad, you were such an amazing friend, and your smiling face always made people feel special.

Foreword

Are you in a position in your life where you want to change your career and learn something new? Are you an entrepreneur at heart? Are you dying to explore other options in life and become a professional success?

Perhaps you would like to get into the animal field. Perhaps you would like to open up a pet grooming business.

If this is the case, you have definitely picked up the right book. *Opening a Pet Grooming Salon* will teach you everything you need to know about opening up a pet grooming business, along with some of the challenges that go along with it. It is an exciting and eye-opening read.

No matter who you are or what your current situation is, regardless of your age, culture, beliefs, or religion, this book is full of insights and will act as a guide in your life, advising you on the steps to take before you make your move and start your new business.

Tanya Ellis has been grooming dogs for the past 23 years. She has owned a successful grooming salon for the last nine years and has made it through a pandemic and many other challenges along the way. In this book, she will share her personal experiences with you to help you overcome fear and will also give you great advice on how to succeed more quickly than she did.

If you want to take your passion for animals to the next level by working in the grooming industry, *Opening a Pet Grooming Salon* will get you started on the right path!

Raymond Aaron
***New York Times* Bestselling Author**

Table of Contents

Chapter 1

How I Got Started

1

My Parents' Basement

My parents' basement is where it all started. I was living with them for the first thirty years of my life, and I started to think about what my passions were. I was always an animal lover, ever since I was a little girl.

My parents allowed me to explore my love for animals, and for all of my childhood life, I had many pets. One of my first pets was a rabbit named Tan-lea, which belonged to my sister Leah and me. (Notice the name was the beginning of each of our names.) We loved this rabbit; she was such a snuggle bug, and she was one of the first animals that we were fully responsible for. We had to take care of her: cleaning the cage, feeding her, and making sure she had water at all times.

Later on, I had another bunny named Cuddles, and she was all mine. She was a grey girl. I was responsible for her all on my own, including the vet bills and everything. I really loved her and remember she was such a fun little bunny. When she was about three, she developed a large tumor on the side of her face. I remember taking her to the vet, and they said that I could have it removed, but it would most likely grow back. They had given me the option to have her put down because otherwise, the tumor would just keep growing and get really big. I was devastated and, as a young girl, had to get advice from the people in my life who cared about me and her. We had her put down, and my heart was crushed.

I was always a dog lover. At first, my parents didn't want us to get a dog because of the responsibility that would come along with owning one, and they knew, being but kids, that we would be the main caregivers of the dog. We were not allowed to have a dog right away, but one day, while we were in Montreal visiting my Opa and the extended family, my dad came home with a boxer puppy. He was a wee puppy, so small he could fit in the palm of my hand. My mom wasn't thrilled with it to begin with, as my dad didn't tell her he was getting a dog. She thought he was going to get a bird.

My sisters and I immediately fell in love and played with him nonstop. My sister had a jacket with the character Wile E. Coyote on it, so I looked at it and said, "Let's name him Wiley," but then we all talked about it and decided that the name Willie was cuter. So, Willie it was.

Willie was a little bundle of joy for us. We couldn't get enough of him. He grew on my mom after a while of being part of our family. Willie was such an amazing dog; he was so smart and loving. For the first seven years of his life, he was rambunctious and excitable; he would always jump over the gate and run to the park, meaning he regularly took off and escaped our backyard.

There were teachers and students at Elmcrest Public School who would call and tell us Willie was there in the field playing with the kids. As I got older, I started doing a lot of training with him and taking him for his long walks, which he required daily. He went through beginner obedience, novice, and advanced training. With a lot of hard work and practice, he passed with flying colors. Since Willie was so

friendly and loving, all our neighbors got to know him well.

Willie was the start of my true love for dogs, and my love continued to grow as time went on.

I remember the day we decided to go on a vacation to Florida. We decided to find a place for Willie while we were on vacation, so we found this place called BRB K9 Services. We came home from our trip and had missed Willie terribly. We came back to get him, and he was happy-go-lucky and so excited to see us, but you could tell he had a great time during his stay there.

My mom was a huge supporter of my big dreams. While we were picking up Willie, she asked the lady who happened to be the owner of BRB, Sherri Davis, if she was hiring any young people. I was standing right next to her, and something magical happened. Sherri, the owner of BRB, said yes, she was hiring. I remember that she gave me her number, and we scheduled an interview.

That moment forever changed my life; my long love of working with animals was about to begin. Sherri said that she was going to give me a chance and see how I worked out and how I would manage becoming part of their team. I'll explain a little more about this chapter in my life later in Chapter 5, under "My First Real Job."

Reading The Secret

When I was younger, I had a lot of insecurities about myself. I was shy, I never talked, and I always had issues about being in large crowds of people. I never wanted my voice to be heard. But secretly, I really did want my voice to be heard. During these insecure years, while living in my parents' basement, I decided that I needed to change something about myself—about how I thought about myself.

I heard of this book called *The Secret*, so I decided to pick up the book and start reading it, and I realized how much I resonated with it. I read through the book line by line, and then it began: the transformation. Everything in this book was slowly starting to make a difference in my life.

Although it didn't happen right away, I started to notice small changes within myself and realized that I could do just about anything if I put my mind to it. We are way more powerful than we ever give ourselves credit for. *The Secret* taught me that you can have anything you want in life if you're willing to work hard.

The Secret became a huge part of my life. I picked up the book whenever I was feeling down and wanted to accomplish something. Not only did it help me in my personal life, but it also helped me a lot in my soon-to-be business life, though business was still quite some time away.

I went through many experiences in my life and lots of different jobs, and I remember someone once saying to me, "Wow, you really change what you're doing a lot." I remember always talking about the possibility of having my own business, but I still had a lot of growing to do before I was going to get there. So, I took every opportunity I could to work with different people so that I could find out what I liked and didn't like, and I ended up learning so much from so many places that I worked for, which I believe was imperative for the work ethic that I have today.

If you haven't read the book *The Secret*, I really suggest you pick it up and give it a good read. It's on my bedside table to this day! It's a constant reminder that anything is possible.

Choosing a Business Name

It's kind of hard for me to remember way back when, but I decided to go with Pooches and Pals. This was the name that inspired me, and I knew it had to be mine. Once I chose the name, I heard from someone that it was a good idea to have it registered with the province so that no one else could take that specific business name, and I remember back then that it wasn't as easy as it is today! You actually had to go to an office, wait in line, and be in front of a person, where you would write down the three choices for different business names that you had. They would then run a search, and you would find out within a few days if any of those names were available.

I remember picking Pooches and Pals, but I'm not sure of the other ones I chose. I found out after the name search was complete—I believe it took three days at that time—that Pooches and Pals was not available. So, I ended up getting my second choice, which was what it is today, Pooches N' Pals. Once you have the business name registered, the fun begins. It was time to create my logo.

I remember this day like it was yesterday. I was doodling on a piece of paper with a pencil, and I came up with a few different ideas. I remember showing my family what I had come up with. I finally had the perfect logo. It just so happens that my neighbor, Steve, had an employee who was in graphic design, and he created my very first logo. The original logo was pink, had five paw pads, and five different animals: a dog, a cat, a guinea pig, a rabbit, and an iguana.

Now that I had the logo, I could start planning marketing tools. At the time, I was working at the Beer Store, and Bill Booth created my first set of marketing tools. He made flyers and business cards, which I still have to this very day. And I remember him saying how interesting it was that my logo looked like a telephone. I never thought about that and how clever that was.

Writing Down My Goals

Something that I've learned and have always taken very seriously is that when you write something down, it tends to come true.

I had vision boards my whole life. It's funny because when you go back, and even if those goals are written in a notebook, and that notebook is buried in your pile of books, you notice how many of those goals actually came true. Writing it down is extremely powerful.

Usher says success is about dedication. You may not be where you want to be or doing what you want to do when you're on the journey, but you've got to be willing to have a vision and foresight that lead to an incredible end.

Walt Disney said, "If you can dream it, you can do it."

I always used to keep a journal, and in this journal, I would write down all of my daily events, how they made me feel, and how I could get better, etc. A journal is something that some people take lightly, but I feel like it's helped me develop as a person. Being shy when I was younger, it really helped me release my feelings in a way that I was able to do at the time.

Making notes is also a great way to implement what you have learned throughout your life and helps to register it in your brain more easily than just listening.

Tony Robbins says, "Setting goals is the first step in turning the invisible into the visible."

Tell Everyone and Anyone

Word of mouth is key in building a business. Originally, it started with friends and family. I told all of them that I was grooming dogs in my parents' basement. I always had other jobs where I worked full-time, so my business always came second. That was what I had to do to get by at the time. I learned a lot from these jobs, including managerial skills, customer service skills, and teamwork skills. I also learned a lot about cleanliness.

I would go around talking to as many people as possible about my business. I would do funny things like going to Starbucks and, instead of saying my name, I would say my business name as the name they would put on the cup. I would go to vet clinics in the area and network with them, as well as the local businesses in the area and the pet stores that didn't have grooming. Basically, everyone that I knew was told what I was up to so that if they knew someone who had a dog that needed grooming, then I was the person that would be top of mind. This really helped me build my part-time business while still working full-time.

It's funny and super cute that my little sister Tiffany's (aka Kidd) friends became my clients a lot of the time. It's so heartwarming, and I will never forget that they came to see me in the very beginning when I was first starting out; when it mattered so much.

Starting a new business is difficult, especially when you're brand new and have a schedule to work with. I was always happy that friends and family would come to me for grooming. It was basically always word of mouth; that's why I talked to anyone and everyone about what I was up to.

Doing Lots of Research

When I was younger, I worked for BRB K9 Services. I kind of knew that that's what I wanted to do with my life: work with dogs. But I had to experiment with many different jobs and opportunities before I made a commitment to do that.

I had many jobs and many opportunities, which made a lot of people in my life question where I was going and what I was doing. I even remember someone saying, "Are you ever going to figure it out?" I laughed and said, "I have no idea." I think, in my heart of hearts, I always knew what I was going to do, but I just wasn't settled enough to make the decision at such a young age!

Some of the jobs that I had when I was growing up were a newspaper route, babysitting jobs, the Oakville Humane Society, Hy and Zel's, the greasy (my friends from Laurentian University will remember this restaurant), Alice Fazooli's, Family Fitness, several vet clinics, many pet grooming salons, the Toronto Zoo, and the Beer Store.

Now, you may be wondering why this is listed under research. Well, because I feel it's important to talk about all of the things that I did before I started my passionate career in pet grooming. All of these things have definitely helped me develop into the person that I am today. Without these experiences, I don't know that I would be on this path and headed in this direction.

I am proud of all the opportunities that I have had in my lifetime. From some of those places I worked, I still have friends to this day, and I'm so grateful to know them.

Each of these places taught me something that I will carry with me forever, and they are things that I implement in my business today. For instance, at one of the places that I worked, the owner was incredibly organized and clean; he didn't tolerate anything less. I really respect that, and it's something that I implement as a policy at Pooches N' Pals today.

Many of my experiences working in the animal industry, and a lot of the research that I did along the way, will stay etched in my mind. I use this information daily.

Chapter 2

Having a Dream

2

Starting Off Somewhere

Getting back to BRB K9 Services, I was really young when I started there, and I was working for Sherri Davis. Sherri was smart and inspiring, and the reason I wanted to start my own business was so that I could be like her. I wanted people to look up to me like they looked up to her. I wanted to feel special and to feel needed. It's where I started off and where I learned so much about myself and my love for animals, especially dogs. She had so much knowledge, and I was a sponge at the time, just wanting to soak up everything and anything I could about dogs. We went to dog shows together, I taught puppy training and novice classes, groomed dogs, answered the phones, provided excellent customer service, cleaned up, and fed the dogs. It was honestly an opportunity of a lifetime for me. They say everything happens for a reason, and it certainly does! I was meant to be there, to learn from Sherri. And something cool about Sherri now is that she is the head trainer of Rex from the TV show *Hudson and Rex*. Congratulations, Sherri, on your amazing achievements.

The second place I worked was my co-op placement in high school. I was at Southdown Animal Clinic, where Doctor Warren was the owner. The placement was one year long, from what I can remember, and there was another veterinarian named Doctor Roberta Vietch. She was like a mentor to me and marked me on my productivity. At this clinic, I learned so much. They cared for animals in such a way that it was admirable. The cleanliness throughout the clinic taught me how important it is to make sure I implement the same thing in my salon.

Pick a Passion

I say "pick a passion" because I speak with a lot of people who are confused about wanting to start a business and have no idea what kind of business to start. For me, it was easy to choose to work with dogs. It was just what I had to do, and it's what I was born to do. There really was nothing else that made sense to me. Sure, I had ideas about other things that I possibly wanted to do, but honestly, it always came back to dogs.

I think that people who want to get into business for themselves need to spend some time really getting to know themselves. What do you always go back to? What makes you happy? Can you see yourself doing this for a living?

Passion is what drives every human on the face of the planet. Donovan Bailey said, "Follow your passion, be prepared to work hard and sacrifice, and above all, don't let anyone limit your dreams."

George William Frederick Hegel said, "Nothing great in the world has ever been accomplished without passion."

Nelson Mandela said, "There is no passion to be found playing small, in settling for a life that is less than the one you are capable of living."

Michael Schumacher said, "Once something is a passion, the motivation is there."

Oprah Winfrey said, "Passion is energy. Feel the power that comes from focusing on what excites you."

And one last quote from Wanda Sykes, who said, "If you feel like there's something out there that you're supposed to be doing, and if you feel a passion for it, then stop wishing and just do it."

This quote really resonates with me because I talk to a lot of people, and they say, "Oh, I should really do that one day," or, "I wish I could do that," or, "You are so lucky," or, "It must be nice." I say this because what I actually did was test the waters a lot when I was young. I figured out what I wanted and what I didn't want. I remember at one point in my life, I wanted to become a veterinarian; however, because I decided to work at places like vets' offices, there were certain parts of the job that I could not deal with, such as putting down animals. I knew that in my heart of hearts, I could never become a veterinarian.

You have to test the waters; you have to figure out what you like to do and what you don't like to do, and whether you can live with some of the things in the job that are going to drive you nuts. Is it the kind of nuts that you can be happy with? With everything in life, there are problems, and you have to remember that! And also remember that hard work is key to success! It's never going to be easy, no matter what!

Passion in art, in coffee, in talking to people and helping people, or writing, or with animals, or with the elderly, are just some examples of passions that you could possibly pursue, and I think that you should follow your heart because your heart always knows the way. If you think too much, your head just gets in the way.

I certainly feel blessed that I found my passion at such a young age, and I feel really blessed that my parents let me be who I am without judgment or questions. Thank you to my mom and dad for letting me live my passion for dogs and sacrificing for me to get better! I love you both so much for that. I'm truly grateful.

Why I Chose Dogs

Well, as you may have already figured out, I had an incredible bond with my boxer, Willie. He and I were like best buds. I would spend a lot of my spare time with him. We went to training classes together and had long walks in the park at Jack Darling Park. We were pretty much inseparable.

I just loved being with Willie, and he pretty much shaped my life. I'm sure many animal lovers will understand when I say this. So, it was only natural that I pursue a career with dogs.

I felt like I connected with dogs in a way that I didn't connect with humans when I was younger. I know this may sound a little odd, but I didn't really fit in much. Don't get me wrong, I had friends that I loved and cared about. But dogs were always there, with a wagging tail to greet me and zero judgment. I felt like I knew it was my calling, but I wasn't completely sure. I had to get through a lot of different times in my life to realize what my true calling was. I always came back to working with dogs, no matter what, so I guess it was meant to be.

I remember when I was in high school and had finished my co-op placement. At the end of the year, I did my final presentation, and it was crazy how much attention I got from fellow students. On second thought, it may have been because I brought a dog to school. I remember feeling so important in that moment. I always had a hard time speaking in front of large crowds, but because I knew about dogs, it was easier to talk and share my passion with the other students. Even though that was a pivotal moment, I still didn't know what I was going to do with my life. But does anyone really know at that age?

So, I continued to experiment through my younger years and worked at many different places with animals to get as much experience as possible. I wanted to gain the knowledge that I would need in order to pursue a career in the animal field.

I was in and out of jobs a lot, always butting heads with someone, but little did I know that one day I would become an entrepreneur. If only I knew then what I know now!

After quite a bit of experience working at different jobs, I began my career by going to school. I took Animal Care at St. Lawrence College in Kingston, Ontario, and then I took a year off to work. It was then that I started working at the Toronto Zoo. After that, I went to Laurentian University. I started off taking science, and I remember the first week feeling defeated, so I decided to switch my major to social science. University was great, and I made a lot of great friends. I learned a lot about myself and university, but I only went for one year and decided it just wasn't for me.

After a few more years of working at different places, including the Beer Store (another great job), I decided that I wanted to get into the animal field. That's when I started working for a large corporation in the animal industry. I worked for PetSmart.

At first, my parents thought I was nuts. I was leaving a job that paid very well and had a lot of security and benefits to go to a lower-paying job. I decided this was just what I needed to do, so it began: my life of working with dogs.

It became very exciting very quickly. I shone in this position and quickly moved up the ladder, becoming a salon manager. I thoroughly enjoyed this position because it really did challenge me, and it made me a stronger leader. I learned so much from this company, and I'm truly grateful that I had the opportunity to learn from them.

After about a year of working for PetSmart, I gave myself a five-year goal. I said that at five years, I would own my own business. Five years came up so quickly, and one day I heard of an opportunity. This opportunity was for me to own my own salon. I had to act quickly. What a life-changing experience this was going to be for me. I remember being terrified but excited at the same time. I had gone from PetSmart, just shy of my five-year goal (*The Secret A*), to being a brand-new business owner, and I felt as if I were walking on hot coals.

Being Inspired

I just love this topic. I have had so many inspirational leaders in my lifetime that I would literally be here all day listing them. A few come to mind, so here we go. I'm going to mention them in no particular order.

During my time at PetSmart, I had a manager named Steve Elliott. This was when I first stepped into my role as salon manager, and I took it on not knowing what I was in for. I was in for the ride of my life. Steve was there every step of the way to guide me through this challenging experience. His leadership skills are second to none, and I am so grateful that I had him as my leader. I really don't think I could have done it without him by my side. He made me believe in myself in times of doubt. Isn't that what any great leader should do? Steve, you taught me so much about the industry and about being a manager; it made my job a whole lot easier.

In my Beer Store days, Willie Dominick was my second manager. He taught me some important things, like saving in Canada Savings Bonds, which I knew nothing about before I worked there. This inspired me to save so that I could have the things I wanted later. I remember one of the things he said to me when I first started there: "I'm giving you three months to prove yourself, and if you can't do that, then you're not the right fit." I really feel this was an amazing way to get someone to do the best job they could. I loved how he led the team more as a friend than as a strict leader. I learned a lot of great customer service skills there, which I took with me for life. I also learned teamwork. Teamwork is something that every human on this planet should learn. After all, Jay Rock says, "Teamwork makes the dream work." This is by far my favorite quote of all time!

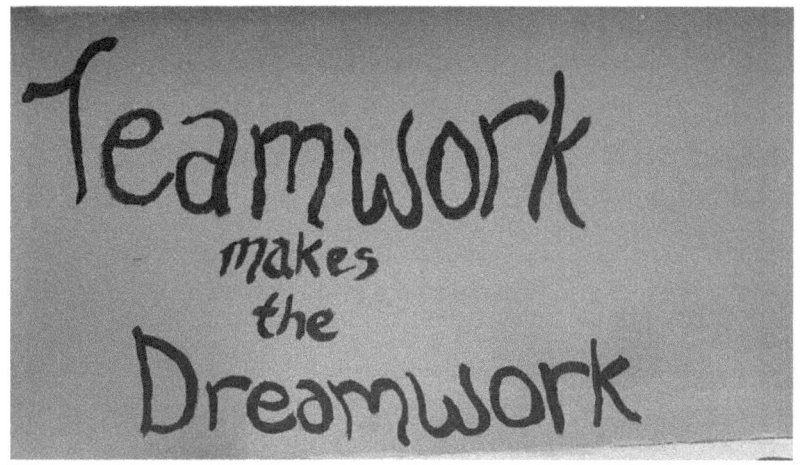

I also found inspiration in reading many positive books on business, leadership, dog grooming, finance, and more. I was always looking for inspiration from somewhere, trying to capture the next great idea. I tried to take things I learned from working with other people and apply them to my own life to try and improve myself.

Usher said, "In life, you have to go through something to get to something. From that, the inspiration comes—having something of substance to talk about; otherwise, you're just considered to be fluff."

In August 2021, I took a Business Mastery course by Tony Robbins. This was such an unbelievable course, and I learned so much. It inspired me to finish this book, as I had started it in 2016, embarrassingly enough. I had an epiphany one morning when I saw that one of my friends, Amy Evans, had finished her book, so I decided that was it. Anthony, my husband, purchased a course called 10-10-10, and we were members, so I decided that it was time to finish my book. This three-day course inspired me to hopefully finish my book in the next couple of weeks. Well, it took three months, but at least it's getting done, finally. Like I said, I look for inspiration everywhere.

Overcoming Rejection

When I found the salon that I was going to take over, I had already given notice to the company that I was with at the time. The bank wanted proof of employment, other than just seeing a bank statement or a pay stub. They wanted to speak with one of the managers to help me out with financing. That day was very strange. I was sitting in the office with the financial advisor, and she was calling my place of employment to get proof that I worked there. I was shaking in my boots. All the managers were in a manager's meeting at that moment.

Unbelievable! Can you even imagine that phone call going through and them all being busy, and the financial advisor saying, "Okay, let's do this"? The bank teller couldn't get through and decided that she was going to go ahead with the loan since she noticed that I had been working and my bank statements showed that I was being paid by my previous employer. The loan went through, and I was able to start my business. My heart felt like it was going to stop, but everything happens for a reason. That's when I knew "the secret" was taking place. My dream of owning my own business was coming true right before my very eyes. God was on my side, and everything was falling into place.

Not only do you have to overcome rejection from financial institutions, but also, when you're starting a business and you get a phone call from a new client, it's hard when they do not move forward, especially when you're starving for business. I hate to say it that way, but in the beginning, every "no" hurts, but at the same time, every "yes" feels amazing! There are ups and downs to running a business, and still to this day, I have hurdles to overcome. It really is all worth it in the end.

Richard Branson said, "You don't learn to walk by following rules. You learn by doing and by falling over."

Gordon Ramsay said, "I don't like looking back. I'm always constantly looking forward. I'm not the one to sort of sit and cry over spilt milk. I'm too busy looking for the next cow."

Julie Andrews said, "When one door closes, another window opens."

As I mentioned previously, I used to work for PetSmart. I was there for just shy of five years. It was one of the highlights of my career, as I learned so much about people, customer service, teamwork, safety of pets, management, and more.

I left my full-time job at the Beer Store to work for PetSmart full time. It was a tough choice, and a lot of people thought I was nuts, but I chose happiness over money. This was where my full-time career began as a pet groomer.

I had a strong love for this company. I was dedicated, hard-working, and I always went above and beyond. I remember the salon manager at the time, who was a super nice person. She saw potential in me. Shortly thereafter, she got pregnant, and it was sort of expected that I would be taking over the role as salon manager. I was only in the job for about six months at the time. They threw me into the fire, but I always feel like that's the best thing to do when you are learning a new position. You learn so much about yourself at the time, and like I said, I had some great managers who worked with me to make sure that I had the support I needed to get the job done.

It was a challenging job as well, and sometimes my team would test me. I felt like I was giving and giving, and I would just get taken advantage of. That was a poor mindset for me to have at the time when I think back. It was important to lay down the law and make sure everyone followed the rules. If you let one person get away with something, it turns into a nightmare.

PetSmart always had the client's interests at heart, which was another reason I enjoyed working there. I took that practice with me into my business, and it has never steered me wrong.

The customer experience and the safety of pets and employees are of utmost importance. Of course, it's never going to be perfect. We're always going to try our best, but sometimes you just can't make someone happy no matter what you do. To be honest, those people just aren't worth it anyway. I hate to say it like that, but sometimes people are just extremely unreasonable. I always find that it's the ones you go above and beyond for that completely take advantage of the situation. I can recall a few situations where we tried our best, and the client was so unimaginably awful to deal with.

One time, this groomer shaved the ears too short because they were matted (she had to). Afterwards, the ear developed a hematoma. A hematoma is a small bruised area that develops at the very end of the ear after it has been shaved. I even remember the dog's name. Can you believe that? It was the end of the day, around a 6:30 p.m. appointment, and the groomer had already bathed the dog and left the dog to sit in a crate for a few minutes. She noticed that the ear was starting to develop the hematoma, so we did what was right. As the salon manager, I took the dog to the vet and had the vet take care of it. We informed the client of the situation.

Unfortunately, the vet was about a half-hour drive away, and because of the time of day, nothing else was open. I mentioned to the vet to take care of the other ear as well because it was also bruising. The vet said no and that it should be okay. Well, of course, when I got back to the salon, the other ear started to bleed as well. Can you imagine?

Unfortunately, these clients were extremely difficult to deal with, and it was an entire family: mom, dad, and two kids. My manager at the time was overly nice to them, offered them drinks from the cooler, and had them sit and wait in the training area. When I returned with the dog, they all completely lost it. They were so incredibly rude.

Prior to grooming, the dog was severely matted from head to toe. I'm guessing you know what matting is. Matting is a condition in your dog's fur that is caused by dense tangles and knots. It's a painful condition that can lead to other health concerns such as skin infections or skin irritations and can also mask other health issues or parasites. Some dogs have coats that are higher maintenance and are more vulnerable to matting.

Now we completely understand that it is an inconvenience when an injury occurs and that your pet means the world to you. We love these dogs, and we don't mean for accidents to occur, but sometimes, unfortunately, they do. Let me tell you, your reaction to the situation can either really help the situation or just make it worse. This has happened multiple times at Pooches N' Pals. We understand that if something happens with your pet in our care, it is not pleasant, and we will take ownership and ask for forgiveness. When this happens, we lose sleep over an injury or incident with a pet in our care.

If I could ask a favor from any client going to see a groomer, it would be this: we know it's hard if we make a mistake, and it can be emotional. Just take a moment and think about how you are going to approach the situation before you react and treat people disrespectfully. Every situation is different, and I'm only speaking on Pooches N' Pals' behalf. We are not evil people, and we do not want to make your lives miserable. We are honest, caring, and compassionate, and we genuinely love your pets. We would love it if you would always let us know how we did after the service, even if you are upset with something, but please be nice about it.

Be kind and be nice, and you will always be treated with the same respect that you give us.

Chapter 3

Hiring the Right Team

3

Trusting People

I've realized over the years that as a business owner, you either trust people or you don't. As soon as you learn to let go and trust, you can have the business that you always dreamed of. When I first started, I had one employee who stayed on with me, and she was a delight. She was great with the dogs and did beautiful haircuts, and it gave me peace of mind knowing that while I was building my business, I already had someone there to service the clients. She was with me for about a year, which was great, but then we parted ways.

At that time, my mom decided to join me part time in the business, helping me wash and dry dogs. It was great having my mom there, and she quickly learned how much she loved it. Mom washed and dried dogs for about two years before I had another groomer come on board part time.

At first, the new groomer was just looking to start up grooming her own client dogs a few days a week, but she ended up wanting a bit more work, so she moved to full time. We became very close, and I totally and completely trusted her. I let her work the shift she wanted, the days she wanted, and groom the number of dogs she wanted. She was with me for quite some time and was even in my wedding party. She had it made.

We had a falling out, and the relationship ended after six years. If she ever reads this book, I do wish her the best of luck in everything she does. She was a huge part of my life, and I'm forever grateful for her being in it. We had some of the funniest times and went through a lot together. We even worked together in other places before she came to work for me.

That year, when our relationship ended, I was going through a terrible personal time in my life, and a lot changed in my business. A lot changed in my life as well. This time in my life was a very big learning lesson for me.

Trusting people isn't easy, but it's a must. Frank Crane said, "You may be deceived if you trust too much, but you will live in torment if you don't trust enough."

Henry L. Stimson said, "The only way to make a man trustworthy is to trust him."

Ronald Reagan said, "Trust, but verify."

It's a great feeling when you can trust someone; it's a feeling of freedom. The more people you trust, the happier you will be, and the happier they will be.

Choosing People for the Right Roles

When I first started Pooches N' Pals, I focused mostly on hiring groomers and bathers. When you're starting a grooming business, this is important.

After the second year, I asked my mom if she wanted to switch roles. My mom went from bather to receptionist. It was a tough transition for me, but it worked out so gracefully, and it really took the business to the next level. Plus, my mom loves serving the clients, and they love her just the same. Mama Bear is what we call her, and that is truly what she is. To this day, clients still tell me they love that they feel a part of the family. It truly is remarkable.

After all, our motto is, "You're family now," but we also have on our website, "Treat others the way you would like to be treated." New clients regularly comment on how they feel so special when they come in. It makes us feel so loved, and I'm so happy that they feel the same way.

We also started hiring co-op students; they help with things such as cleaning, bathing, drying, and more. We have hired other roles as well, such as a media person and an accountant. After almost nine years, we now have groomers, bathers, groomer trainees, a receptionist, an operations manager, and a district manager. My role has changed from groomer to business owner, teacher, author, and web designer, pretty much overnight.

When you find people to do the right roles, they flourish in those roles. You find their true passions, and it keeps them happy. We are currently looking for another media person and would like to find a veterinarian and a dog trainer to join our team.

Doing the Job Yourself to Begin With

When you first start your business, you wear many hats. You are the manager, the groomer, the complaint department, the receptionist, the handyman or woman, the window cleaner, the cleaning person, the social media person, the web designer, the marketing director, the hiring manager, and the operations manager. You do it all yourself!

I feel that in the beginning, it's important to take on all these roles because if you learn the roles, you learn how to teach other people how to perform the roles. Taking on all these roles in the beginning requires a lot of time and energy, and basically, your workday is never-ending (at least 12-hour days every day for the first three years—who am I kidding, I mean eight years). Don't get me wrong, it's very rewarding building a business from being so small to being where it is now. It took a lot of effort, but I wouldn't change it for anything. I wouldn't go back. I would do it again in a heartbeat!

I feel these steps are part of the learning process of building the business, plus you realize just what you're good at and what you don't like to do, and you can hire the right people to do the jobs you are not so good at.

Recently, in a Tony Robbins Business Mastery seminar, he talked about being an entrepreneur, an artist, and a business owner. He makes you realize who you are and what you should focus on. Funny thing is, Tony Robbins is an artist as well, and he loves speaking in front of large audiences. That is his true passion—helping people. When you realize what you're good at, you shine. It's quite magical to watch people in their true passions.

The fun part about doing it yourself is that it turns out to be very rewarding and humbling because you know that when you start to succeed in life, you are the one who did it, fought the good fight, worked hard, played hard, and kept going no matter what. You get to be a role model for other people who work with you and become your teammates. They'll all see that you did it all too!

Don't Expect Perfection

I've always had high expectations of the people I hire. I expect a lot from my team. Perfection is something that I've always strived for.

"Shoot for the moon.
Even if you miss, you'll land among the stars."

– Brian Littrell

I always keep this quote in the back of my mind, which leads me to this: perfection is overrated. Nothing is perfect, no one is perfect, so striving for perfection is not something I do anymore. I've learned over the years to accept people for who they are. I allow them to grow at a pace that works for them. Everyone is different. I love the uniqueness of everyone I meet; it's fun to watch people grow and develop in their roles.

I've gone through many changes throughout the years with Pooches N' Pals' many different teams. It has made me understand the way different people work and that we all have different personality types. I learned, through my husband, about these different personality types, and it's really helped me understand how each person on my team operates. The personality types are action, stability, theory, and relationship.

The action personality type is a person who loves adrenaline, hitting goals, and making history. The stability type person needs clarity and organization. The theory person loves facts and solving problems. The relationship person loves people and being part of something special. Usually, most people have one strong personality type mixed with a couple of the other ones, or just one of the other ones. I feel that once you know your personality types, it's easier to understand how you learn and grow. Once you start figuring out what other people's personality types are, it helps you understand them better, and you can then help them grow and develop into the person they want to become. This is remarkable in the sense that no two people are the same.

When I meet someone, it takes me a few weeks to figure out what their personality type is. Once I figure it out, I know exactly what they need. Being a business owner and a team player, this quality of knowing personalities is extremely important in developing relationships with others.

I have never again expected perfection from anyone; however, I do feel that expecting people to be their best selves is extremely important. Having a higher expectation of yourself will make you shoot for higher goals and will help you develop as a person.

Find People with the Same Passion

I learned over the years that finding people who had the same passion as myself was extremely important. I didn't want to hire people who just wanted a job. I wanted to find people who had a passion for animals and wanted to become possible groomers or bathers so that the energy in the salon would always be about the dogs and the clients having a great environment to be in.

Passionate people always shine through; they make it better at work. They make going to work fun. I focused on this because it helped grow my team. It's great when you have these fun people that you're surrounded by, with whom you have so much in common and can do things together.

In the past, with my sort of original team, we would do fun things such as going to grooming shows together. We would go on outings together, attend concerts, and they would attend all of my family gatherings and social events. We were like a family. This is a catch-22 because it's sometimes hard to manage people when you treat them like family.

A good place to find passionate people is through schools. I always looked to hire co-op students because I remember when I was young and wanted an opportunity. There were many employers who gave me that opportunity, and I'm so grateful. If they hadn't given me a shot, I wouldn't be where I am today. It's been great finding those passionate people to work with and train. Even when I worked for a major corporation, I remember hiring people who later became business owners and animal lovers all around the GTA. I love inspiring and helping others find their passion. This is one of my passions!

Not only is it important to find people who are passionate, but you also have to find the right role for that person. Some people are good with working hands-on (refer to personality types). Every person is so different, and finding the different roles over the years has become something that I'm very good at. My mom used to work as a bather for me, and then about three years in, we decided that she would become the receptionist. My mom was the main greeter of the business, and clients just loved her. Of course, they would—who wouldn't?

It was a transition, and I had to find someone new to become a bather with me. But it all worked out. That's when I found Monika. Monika started off as a bather for quite some time, and she developed into a groomer over the years. Now Monika is a groomer and still works with me to this day. I'm so grateful for Monika; we found each other through the YMCA program 8.5 years ago. Thank you, Monika, for sticking with me. I appreciate you a lot. Monika was one of the only ones during COVID-19 who stuck by my side through everything. We worked when no one else wanted to.

Delegate to Others

When I first took over Pooches N' Pals, I remember there was a girl who had already worked there. The previous business owner said that there wasn't enough work for two people in that salon, but I spoke with the employee and asked her if she wanted to continue working there, and she said yes. We worked together for about a year. Having someone working as a groomer allowed me to concentrate on building the business. When you have your own business, it's important to have others work for you and with you.

Delegating has always been easy for me. I have always been able to trust people until they let me down. It happens, and it's a part of business. It builds strong character, that's for sure.

Since my days of working for a large corporation, I've always loved working in a team; it has always been something that I've enjoyed. You get to work with so many kinds of people with so many different personality types, and every person can teach you something. They can also add a lot to your business that you didn't even know was a possibility.

Right now, I'm literally sitting on my couch writing my book, and I have two functioning salons. Never in my wildest dreams did I ever think this would be a possibility. I am so incredibly grateful for my teams. You all know who you are. It has been a pleasure working with every one of you.

We took over Pooches in the Bluffs, which used to be Anni's Mutt Cutts, on September 1, 2021. The owner and I have been friends for a long time; we used to work together at a big-box chain. When we worked together at PetSmart, she was a manager there, and she fell in love with grooming when I was the salon manager. I remember the day like it was yesterday. She approached me about becoming a groomer, and the rest is history. She became an amazing groomer. She worked in the salon caring for dogs as if they were her own.

Years later, she took over a salon in the Bluffs. She owned and operated her business for three years. The COVID-19 pandemic hit and was tough on everyone. She had a lot of traumatic things happen in her life, so she thought of selling her business. At first, I didn't think I would want another business, but I knew what kind of person she was, and I knew I wanted to help her. I thought this was a great opportunity to help her and take on a new adventure. So far, it has been great. The team there is awesome, and it is self-sufficient and running smoothly.

Chapter 4

Taking Massive Action

4

Daily Steps to Making It Happen

What I mean by taking massive action is taking small steps every day towards your end goal, and this means remaining focused on whatever you do. For example, doing one thing every day towards your business goal is crucial to building a business. Even when you're working full time, you should always make time for your business. You should never be too tired or too busy. I remember taking small steps, whether it was making business cards or creating a website or starting an email address or telling my friends about what I was doing. Once you start telling people, then you better believe that they're going to hold you accountable. This will keep you motivated to continue your journey to opening your business. There will be bumps in the road; there will be good days and bad days, but if you do one small task every day, you will remain on track to the end goal.

For the last eight years, I have woken up almost every morning at around 3 a.m. to write down my ideas. This really helps the potential of my business. Don't get me wrong, I'm not telling you to do exactly that. It's just something that became a habit for me. Every night, I would go to bed dreaming about my next steps. I found the best way for me was to wake up from that dream and write down my idea. You must keep a journal next to your bed to do this, but don't wake up your partner. Bring your journal to the bathroom if you must.

Every small action that you take is one step closer to the big dream. Don't worry if one day you don't take an action; it's okay, but try to get back on track as soon as possible. Every time you don't do that one small thing, you're further away from your goal.

Some things I do at 3 a.m. are update my website, create great content for social media, and schedule my posts for Facebook and Instagram. I think of new ways to improve my business, more ways to market my business, and new fun things to do for my business. There is always a task that can be done.

I believe I am super business oriented; I love helping people start a business. This is one thing that I can add as value to you, whether it's a pet grooming business or any business. I'm great at brainstorming ideas, so if you'd like to connect with me on that level, I'd be more than happy to help you start your business. If you would like to connect with me, please add me as a friend on Facebook: Tanya E. Ierullo.

Or email me directly at information@poochesnpalsinc.com or find me on Instagram: instagram.com/poochesnpals.

Starting a Website

A website is super important when starting a business. It lets people know what you are doing. It's one of the ways that you can start becoming branded. On your website, you should list things that you do as a service. A lot of people think that starting a website is difficult. Honestly, it's one of the easiest things you can do for your business if you're looking for something that's easy and has simple content with wording. I am great at this, and I have instructed others on completing their own websites. If you ever need help with that, reach out to me on Facebook: Tanya E. Ierullo, or by email at information@poochesnpalsinc.com.

If you want help building a website that's easy to maintain, I can definitely help, with one free session on who to use and how to get started. You can literally edit your website in about three minutes or less, as long as you know what you want to put up and how to change it. I've learned throughout the years that being innovative and up to date with your content on your social media and website keeps you ahead of the game.

It's odd how some businesses refuse to get on social media and start current, modern, up-to-date websites. I personally do not understand this mentality, as it has not worked for many businesses. During the COVID-19 pandemic, I heard that many businesses perished. Maybe they weren't innovating. Maybe they weren't ready for change, or maybe they didn't know where to look for help. I am not knocking anyone here, and I personally don't really know the circumstances that other business owners experienced. The pandemic was a tough time and continues to be a struggle. I was born ready. I thrive on change.

Pooches N' Pals won an award in 2021 called the Consumer's Choice Award. In a nutshell, what they do is ask consumers who the best businesses are in every market. The Consumer's Choice Award is a well-recognized award, established in 1987 in Montreal, and is now coast to coast in 28 cities. Once they have found the best in each and every market, they develop marketing programs each and every year around the fact that those companies have been chosen by consumers as being the best at what they do. The selection process is what they are most proud of, and it is unlike any other award company; they solely rely on third-party research marketing groups. There is only one winner in each category, so you, and you alone, can make the claim that you have been chosen by consumers as being the best at what you do. It's the ultimate reinforcement of that purchase decision. Consumers want to do business with a company that other consumers have said is the best. You may be asking yourself what the Consumer's Choice Award has to do with websites. Well, it always looks good to display your awards on your website.

Being Active on Social Media

Nowadays, being active on social media is key to running a business. You can't go without it. Social media will put you in the eyes of your community. People love to see what you're doing; they love to get to know you on a deeper level. I started it as soon as I had my business, way back in 2013. It took my business to a new level.

Facebook was what I was familiar with, and it was where I started with social media. I created a page for my business and invited all my friends, family, and community to follow me to see what my business was up to. Creating fun content to keep people engaged is exciting, and it will regularly get you new business with very little effort.

I could write a book on social media and how it really changed my business for the better. It's good to get confident with making videos and great photos of cute dogs or whatever it is that you do. The rules are always changing on Facebook, so it's good to keep up with the latest trends.

Instagram became my next social media platform to learn. I learned from many people who helped me along. Sue B. Zimmerman, the Instagram expert, is one of my favourite Instagrammers. I took one of her classes, and it really inspired me and taught me a lot about the platform. Since she is an expert, she will keep up with the latest trends and relay those trends to you. I highly recommend her. Her Instagram handle is theinstagramexpert.

I've gained so many clients from Instagram. I love this platform. I highly recommend that you get very comfortable with using it and find out everything you can. The worst that can happen is that you make mistakes on the way, but you can always learn from those mistakes and just keep getting better. The other day, my dad said to me, "Your videos have gotten so good." I'd have to say that it's because I've been practicing a lot.

Recently, I started with TikTok. I haven't really gotten the hang of it yet; I'm still learning and trying. I love TikTok because I feel like the content is so unique and fun to watch. I have a few grooming friends who are great at TikTok. There is a groomer I follow called "girl with the dogs." She was, I believe, one of the original dog groomers that started with TikTok, and she's literally killing it on there. She has over five million followers, and her content is so real and informative. I love watching her stuff.

The best thing about all of these different platforms is that each one appeals to a different person, age group, and niche. Whatever one you choose is the best one for you. One thing I learned from Sue B. Zimmerman is that creating content that has substance is better than just posting to post. I love social media. You should too.

Creating a Business Plan

Creating a business plan is key before you decide you want to open an actual business. There are many free business templates; if you Google it, you can find one that's easy to use. I created my first business plan when I was about 16 years old. So that's what I did, and guess what? It was the best thing I ever did. I took a huge risk, and now, after nine years, I can pretty much get all the financing I need anytime I want. That's the basic reality of creating a business plan.

Banks and investors need to see that you have a concrete plan on how you expect to run your business so that they can trust that you will be able to repay the money they lend you to start your business. If you think about it logically, it makes sense, right? No one's going to give you money for free unless you prove to them that you can pay it back. They also want to know what the timeline is for payback.

One of my favourite shows is Dragon's Den. These entrepreneurs go on the show and plead their business plan to business owners who are extremely successful, in hopes of becoming partners with them. They can use their expertise, knowledge, and money to make their business better or to start their business from scratch. I've seen the greatest businesses come out of this show. So, if you want to go big, audition for this show.

Creating a business plan doesn't have to be so serious; it can be fun and exciting. Remember, it's the first step in laying down the foundation to your big dream.

Have Others Keep You Accountable

I often tell my friends and family what I'm up to, and that way they can keep me accountable on my goals and dreams. They don't judge me because I change my mind a lot, and that's okay. Sometimes it's more motivating when others keep you accountable, and it's always on the top of their mind because they know what you're up to. If you're having a moment where you're feeling like you're not motivated, as soon as that conversation comes up, it may spark your interest to get going again.

The other day, I was having a conversation with Anthony, my husband. I tend to focus on a lot of different things at once. With my action personality, this is not unusual. The conversation was, "Why don't you just focus on getting your book finished? And then after that, we can get started on that other project you want to do." I had to thank him for keeping me focused because the next day, I got one full chapter done. When you fall off the horse, just remember not to be too hard on yourself. It's going to happen sometimes, but get right back up on that horse and keep going.

Try to have one or two people to keep you accountable. My husband is great at this; he always knows how to pick me up when I'm down. Maybe it's your family, or maybe it's a close friend; maybe it's a colleague or someone you look up to.

When I was younger, I remember talking to friends and family, and this was when I didn't know what I wanted to do with my life, and the same questions always came up: Have you met anyone? What are you up to? What's new? I remember always dreading these questions. This was when I was really shy and basically had no plans for my life. It was always tough to say, "Oh, not much." I feel a lot of those people kept me accountable when I had nothing going on. They were actually preparing me to show them that I am somebody. It feels good now to step into a room and be so confident with who I am. I love that feeling, and all it was, was taking baby steps towards big giant goals. I'm always up to something now. I need to stay busy to keep myself occupied, and I'm always striving for the next goal.

Believe You Can

"If you believe in yourself, anything is possible."

- Miley Cyrus

No one's going to write the book for you. No one's going to hold your hand. No one's going to run the fastest mile for you. You must do those things yourself. The funny thing is, sometimes people won't believe in you right away. The trick is trying to stay positive when you know that some people may not think it's possible for you to achieve your wildest dreams. You must prove that you can do something remarkable for someone to see that you're capable. Sometimes you must do it repeatedly, and that's okay. Eventually, you will have an audience that truly believes in you as you do in yourself.

There have been many naysayers in my life, but I find it really funny how I always proved them wrong. I love the feeling of accomplishing something that is just so farfetched and turns heads. For example, some people from my past, who knew I wanted to start my own business but didn't really believe in me, asked me why I hadn't done it yet. To be honest, sometimes I didn't even have the proper answer. I just knew that I would eventually get it done. I started slowly going through my life and building up a part-time business under the radar. It was very low key. I wanted to keep it that way so that the ones who were non-believers would ignore me. It's better to be that person who shines later. Little did they know, it was years in the making. It really does take practice, meditation, determination, and a whole lot of positivity to keep believing in yourself.

Unfortunately, the world is filled with negativity, but you must constantly read books and positive blogs. Do things like Tony Robbins' priming exercise, which will help you stay focused on your goals and help them come true. I haven't gotten into the habit of priming daily, but when I do, it's crazy. On those days, I have the most success in my business. For example, when we decided that we were going to sell raw food for dogs. In priming, you picture yourself as already having done it, as one of the exercises. When you live in the state of already having done it, you feel the pleasure of the food being sold and of getting your first customer. It's kind of like when an Olympian imagines going through the run. They picture finishing the race and the feeling they get when it's done. That's how I can explain priming, but if you don't believe me, go ahead and check it out. You can find Tony Robbins' priming exercise on YouTube; just type in "priming by Tony Robbins." I truly recommend you do this every day.

If you don't believe in yourself, then who will. I heard a story about Disney once. I believe it was from Tony Robbins again. He said that a reporter had said to Walt Disney's brother, after Walt had passed away, that it must be bittersweet knowing that Walt Disney never got to see Disney being completed. His brother then replied, "Well, that's pretty ridiculous. He had the vision and saw Disney before anyone else did." Powerful, right? It goes to show you how Walt Disney believed in himself, and he also had many others who believed in his dream, which came true. It was probably better than anyone could have ever imagined.

You can literally do anything you put your mind to. This is what I've learned through reading The Secret. As I mentioned before, the book The Secret changed my life in more ways than one. I hope you get the chance to read it one day; it is an easy read and should only take a couple of days to get through. I would love to hear if it resonates with you. Send me a message on Facebook (Tanya E. Ierullo) or Instagram (poochesnpals).

Chapter 5

Experience in the Field

5

Taking Co-op in High School

This was my co-op placement. I remember it like it was yesterday. I chose to do my placement here because originally I had thought that I wanted to become a veterinarian. So I figured I would get as much experience as possible in the animal clinic environment so that I would know what it was all about. Don't get me wrong, I loved it there. However, I quickly realized that this was not the path for me. I definitely learned a lot about how to properly care for an animal through a vet's perspective. I realized how important veterinary medicine is. There were just some aspects of it that I didn't quite enjoy. It was really hard to deal with emergency situations when it came to pets. The staff and team over at Southdown were incredible. They took great care of the pets. I learned a lot about vaccines, flea and tick prevention, dental care, spay and neuters, skin issues, bloat, and more.

I remember that Doctor Veitch, who now works at Erin Mills Pet Hospital, used to be the one who gave my weekly progress reports. I think I still have them. I did fairly well. Co-op is something that I recommend any student do if they want to get experience in a field that they are unsure of or are passionate about. It gives you an opportunity to feel like an employee within a company while being able to learn.

Reading is really important; however, hands-on experience, for me, was a crucial part of my learning. Another very important skill that I learned from that placement was the importance of cleanliness. Southdown was a member of the AAHA, which stands for the American Animal Hospital Association. They offer the highest standards to ensure that veterinary hospitals have the staff, equipment, medical procedures, and facilities required for pet care.

When I was in high school, I decided to take co-op as one of my electives. It changed my life for the better. I was always an introvert. I was so shy, and I literally couldn't speak in crowds at all. I was so nervous to be in large groups of people, and I would get so much anxiety thinking about it that sometimes I just talked myself out of it. To make a long story short, these were the beginning years of my life when I needed to change something. Taking co-op brought me into the world of the hands-on learner, which is what I required. I feel that co-op also teaches responsibility, how to show up on time, and how to be disciplined and open to learning new things. I was so grateful for the opportunity to be able to participate in a co-op program.

Studying is fine but doesn't work for me. My co-op was at Southdown Animal Clinic. I was able to work for volunteer hours, and it was a very rewarding experience for me. I learned all kinds of things about how to care for pets. I learned everything from proper vaccines to grooming, to customer service, cleanliness, teamwork, time management, x-rays, autoclave, proper sanitization, feeding and watering animals, before and after surgery prep care, productivity, and more. There was just so much learning involved; I was never bored, and I couldn't get enough of it. I did well as a student; my marks were impeccable and I shone.

I remember doing my final project. I was able to bring a dog with me to high school, and it was probably one of the more popular displays that any of the students put on that year. I was so impressed with myself and how I started to come out and be more confident. It made me feel special and important. It was easy to talk to people about something that I was passionate about, even though they were probably just there to see the dog.

If you do something you love, it's so incredibly awesome, and people see you in a different light. They may not know the potential you have, but it is certainly believable and needs no convincing. It's okay to be different; it's okay to be unique; it's okay to be shy; it's okay to be unpopular. To be honest, it's probably better to be Rudolph.

Co-op gave me an experience that was unforgettable. I remember Dr. Veitch used to give me my marks every week to track my progress within the clinic. It was always great to hear feedback on how I was doing. I feel that if your leader doesn't do this for you, how are you supposed to get better? Constructive criticism always helps.

My First Real Job

Going back to when I worked for Sherri Davis from BRB K9 Services, she was the first person who ever hired me on, and it was because of my mom that I got the job. As I previously mentioned, we took our dog Willie there for boarding when we went away on a holiday; most likely, we had gone to Florida. When we came back, we picked up Willie, and my mom had asked if I could have the job. Sherri had asked me if I had any experience working with dogs, and I said no. She hired me anyway. She gave me a shot, and she believed in me. And so it began: my love for dogs. This first job was a pivotal moment in my life.

I admired Sherri's character; she was someone I wanted to be like when I grew up. I admired her mentorship. She had so much knowledge of dog behaviour. Also, she had a lot of raving fans, her clients. It was so admirable. I remember thinking how important she was, how everyone would ask for her, and it was the greatest thing in the world. I wanted that exact same respect.

Everyone needs a mentor, someone to look up to. I still look up to Sherri and everything that she has accomplished to this day. Sherri always wanted to train a dog for movies, and she did little bits here and there.

When I worked for Sherri, I was truly blessed to have the opportunity to be able to learn from someone like her. Training was so much fun and was very rewarding. I especially loved puppy class. When all the puppies would finish their training, they would get to be social. This was where Sherri would assess the behaviours of the puppies. She could pinpoint the very shy dog, the aggressive dog, the social dog, and more. It was so much fun to watch and learn. The puppies taught me an incredible amount about dog behaviour, and I just couldn't get enough of it.

I also had the chance to learn how to groom through Sherri, which little did I know would become my passion many years later. She took me to dog shows, where we could watch the dogs being shown in the ring and see who the best dogs were so that breeders could get recognized. I worked for Sherri for a while before I started my co-op placement. I had been given the opportunity to work with Sherri during my co-op placement, but because I wanted more knowledge in the field of dogs, I decided to go to the vet clinic instead.

My experience working for BRB K9 was a great one, and I'll always be truly grateful for the opportunity that I was given, for little old me to find my true passion and become the person that I was meant to be.

Going to College

I went to St. Lawrence College in September 1998. I can't believe it was that long ago. The program that I took was Animal Care. I remember how nervous I was going away to school, wondering what it would be like. It turned out that I wrote a journal to my mom while I was in school, and as I'm reading it now, it's so funny the things that I would tell her. My memory isn't so great. My first journal entry to my mom was Friday, September 18th, 1998, so that's about two weeks into school. I wrote about some of my friends that I had met.

I stayed in residence, and I remember participating in frosh week. I didn't write about frosh week in the journal. But I did read that I used to go for a daily jog. I also was part of the volleyball team when I was in college. In my journal to my mom, I wrote, "I want you to know that if it weren't for you, I would not be here, and if you were not around, then I could not survive without you. To me, you are my guardian angel, and I love you with all of my heart and all of my soul. You are the wind beneath my wings, and you are the reason I wake up every day." Aw, that's so cute.

Going to college really took me out of my comfort zone. I made friends very easily, but before college, I was more of an introvert. I did always have friends... don't get me wrong... but I always stuck to a small group of friends.

College gave me structure and kept me busy. I had to wake up early. A typical day was 7 a.m. Usually, classes began at around 8:30 and went to 11 a.m., and then I had a co-op placement at the Humane Society from 2:30 to 4:40. After that, I had volleyball from 5:05 to 6:45 p.m.

During college, near the end, we got to pick a co-op placement of our choice. I remember one of the teachers mentioning several different places, but what stuck out to me was the Toronto Zoo. I decided that I wanted to do my co-op placement there. I had given them a call, and they ended up calling me back. I got an interview with them. I was so lucky that I ended up getting my placement.

So I got the chance to work in the health unit at the Toronto Zoo, and it was an incredible experience. I got to work with animals such as reindeer, a hornbill, a red panda, a mandrill, and a baby lion, and I got to hand and bottle feed the reindeer and baby lion.

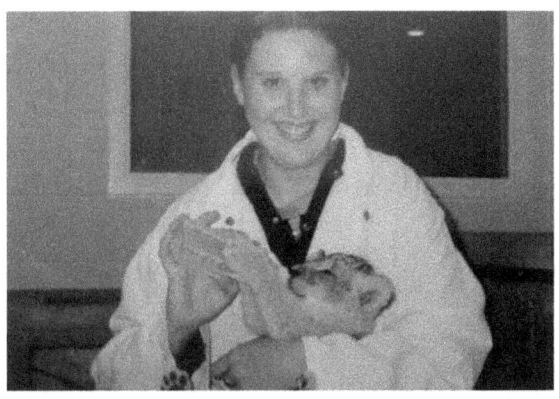

In the second semester, I was taking a grooming course, and I remember completing a grooming project, which I still have to this day. I also took some other courses as extras: sign language, which I was really good at, and criminology, which was interesting.

College was a great balance of schoolwork and fun; I made a lot of friends, and I did a lot of partying. There were a couple of bars that I remember going to, called Stages and AJ's. My friends and I spent a lot of time there. We also played games and hung out in our rooms; we cooked together, we shopped together, and we had movie nights. It was a ton of fun. The friends that I made, we were all in Animal Care together. We spent lots of time together.

I'll always remember this as being a great part of my life, and if your kids have a chance to do it, I highly recommend it. Go to college not just for the school part, but also for the friends that you'll make and the experiences that will mold you into an independent you. It will give you a chance to come out of your shell and be able to make decisions based on what you want and not what your parents want. No offense, Mom and Dad; I love you both (Xo). It will also give you a new respect for your parents, because you have to do your own laundry, cook for yourself and clean up after yourself. No one's going to wake you up and tell you that you have to get to class. These are all really important skills to learn. No one's going to baby you; it's all on you. Make it count every moment.

Going to University

I went to Laurentian University. University was two years after college. I took a year off in between to earn money so that it was less detrimental to my financial situation. I was considered a mature student at that time. I had my own room; it was a corner room for a single student. It was nice, but at the same time it was different, because I didn't have a roommate, and usually the bonds that you make in school start first with your roommate. I participated in frosh week, which really took me out of my comfort zone. We had to do some crazy stuff, like lots of alcohol, weird games and odd wake up times, but you know what? That's where you meet some awesome people, because you're all doing the exact same thing. We had common areas, like the TV room and the kitchen, and there was a shared bathroom for the ladies on our floor, which was something that made me uncomfortable, having to do my business where other people were also.

University was also a good balance of fun and education. I remember starting off the semester going into sciences in hopes of becoming a veterinarian. After the first week, I quickly realized that I found biology, physics and mathematics to be extremely difficult, which would make for a very long semester. The school offered the option of switching majors. So, I changed my major to social science instead. I ended up taking courses such as anthropology, psychology and others I was much better at.

I also remember being physically active during university. I joined the local gym, which was just a hop, skip and a jump away from my residence, and I would regularly go and work out. I didn't put on the regular "freshman 15," the weight gain that usually occurs in college and university from eating habits and drinking habits. Luckily, I did my best to stay fit. I still did partake in a lot of the usual activities and parties, but it was an equal balance.

I do remember being a starving student, buying food such as good old Kraft Dinner, Mr. Noodles and TV dinners, and these would be my food choices throughout the year. I was always missing the home cooked meals from Mama Bear and Papa Bear. I had a car when I was in university, which made things a bit easier, not having to take the bus to get groceries, and I could drive home whenever I wanted. I only went for one year, but that was enough for me. I realized that learning in this manner wasn't how I learn best. Hands-on was always my best option. I made a lot of good friends but decided later that year that I wouldn't go back. At that point, I had started working part time. I do feel as if it was a great experience, and I highly recommend it.

Learning from Other Business Owners and Managers

I find it hard to remember everywhere that I worked. It was to the point where I was bobbing around from workplace to workplace, so much so that some people had said to me, and this always stuck in my head, "Are you ever going to find somewhere and stick with it?" It kind of makes me laugh to this day, because I've always been like that, to the point that it was extremely frustrating at times.

Every place I've worked, I've always listened to the business owner or the managers. I tried to pick out things I liked and disliked from their ways of running a business.

I always seemed to have a problem with the way people ran their businesses. Sometimes everything was terrible, and sometimes it was just some things, and sometimes it was the way people treated others. I always did find some good where I was working. I would take these learning lessons and run away with them, meaning that I would jot them down for a later date. Learning all these things really helped me in my quest to own my own business. It gave me a foundation that I could work with.

I would always pick managers' and business owners' brains for information. I had a burning desire to learn. Some of the tips and tricks that I took away were to do with cleanliness, how to stay organized, how to cash out people, data entry and customer service (which was a big one). These are all important aspects of running a business.

Each opportunity that I had, I can honestly say that I'm truly grateful that I had it. Each experience was unique and really helped me shape my personality and gave me the mental toughness that I needed to run my own business successfully. It didn't all come right away; it has been a work in progress, and it always will be. I keep learning from other business owners and reading as much as possible so that I can have the business of my dreams.

Something I learned early on from business owners was that I needed an accountant. My accountant, Peggie, has been a godsend. It's been nine years in business, and honestly, if it weren't for her, I don't know where I'd be. She always kept me on track, helping me figure out my taxes, my payroll and my income statements at the end of the year. It has been necessary to running a business, and this is one of the most important skills that any business owner can have. Another thing I have learned is to give discounts. Most people in my industry don't really believe in giving discounts; however, I've been the complete opposite for my entire career. I've always believed that if you reward your regular clients, they will want to come back time and time again.

Sometimes I crave the opportunity to work for someone else so that I can learn something new. Right now, I currently have an opportunity where I'm doing something different, and I'm truly excited about it. It's 2021, a year of change.

Chapter 6

Having Business Mentors

6

Within Your Industry

I have always had the opportunity to work with people within my industry and have been able to reach out anytime and schedule learning opportunities to get better with breeds of my choice. For instance, I often reached out to competitors who were more advanced than I was to get better at poodles. I would go to their salons, and they would watch as I groomed a poodle. They would give me tips and tricks on how to make the trim better. This is a great way to learn, because when you're working on a dog that you're familiar with, you can follow the lines next time. Some of my mentors have been Nadia Bongelli, who is recognized as one of the top competitive groomers in our industry, and Priscilla Suddard, from whom I've learned so much over the years, and who has also supported some of the events I have put on.

Isabella Jane Doblas Jones came from Spain, and I hosted her at my salon to teach my team some tips and tricks. I also hosted her at a hotel to give a seminar, and there were groomers who participated and got hands-on experience, grooming their chosen dog and receiving help with their breed. It was awesome.

When I go to grooming competitions, there are many groomers there that I learn from (too many names to mention). The judges will often come over after the grooming competition and look over your dog and give you any tips on how to make the groom better. The suggestion is always that you stay to get that critique, and it has helped me grow to become a better groomer.

I used to be so shy, but not at grooming shows. I always felt like myself there. It was fun because you could make so many friends within the industry and help each other along the way. There are lots of different shows within Canada and the US, which I have attended in the past. During COVID-19, there hasn't been much other than online, which just isn't the same.

If you want to find a great mentor, I suggest going to some of these shows and meeting some new friends. It's always a relaxed environment, and you can eat lunch together and watch the grooming competition together. It's especially great for a newer groomer just starting out, because this industry is tough, and there is so much to learn. You will learn more and will find people with things in common with you, and the best part is that you can always stay in touch on social media. There are groomers that I follow on social media, whom I have never met, one being Jess Rona. I love her Instagram account. It's fun to learn from her. Thank you, Jess, for providing great material and courses for groomers to learn continuously. I've also found other great mentors within grooming groups on social media, specifically on Facebook. You can also just get great tips and tricks from other groomers on how to make your grooms better. I try to stay in positive, uplifting groups.

Having mentors will help you grow and succeed faster and easier.

Outside of Your Industry

I have so many mentors outside of my industry, which I believe help me grow faster. Whenever I get a chance, I attend a seminar, and that helps me grow in some way or another. My husband has a part-time business, and they often host seminars and learning events. I tend to go to as many as possible. I've met some incredible, successful people at these events. Even though it isn't my industry, I'm still able to pick up many different tricks for my business; it's all somewhat relatable. Plus, it's always positive and inspiring. When you're around happy people, it's contagious.

I remember a seminar that I went to several years ago. Some of you may know it; it was called "Landmark." This course was very intense and lasted for several days, and it helped me get to the bottom of an issue that I was struggling with for quite some time. I'm not going to get into the nitty gritty details of it; however, if you are struggling with something that's holding you back, taking one of these courses will help you overcome that limiting belief. This seminar involved a lot of group activity, so you had to get into groups and talk over what it was that you were struggling with, and share how you would help each other overcome it. I guess you could say it's kind of like positive therapy in a way.

Everyone needs someone to talk to and figure things out. Everyone needs great mentors to help them lead their way. I admire Hazel McCallion, the mayor of Mississauga for many years, an incredible woman who just celebrated her 100th birthday on February 14th. I also admire Tony Robbins, world speaker, and Anthony Ierullo, my husband and life partner.

This year, because of the COVID-19 pandemic, has obviously been a tough year for everyone. I tried my hardest to stay as positive as possible, but when you're running a business, it's obviously more difficult than anyone can imagine. I'm lucky that I have a great husband. He helps guide me, and he provides me with so much support, and more times than once has walked me back from the edge of the cliff. My husband is the most supportive; he is my rock, and he lifts me up in more ways than one.

I decided to take Tony Robbins' "Unleash the Power Within" course in June. I rented a small room in Blue Mountain where I could be alone and take the online course, so that there were no distractions. I had no idea what it was going to be like, but the energy was unbelievable, and I can't even begin to describe what a life changing event this was for me. It gives you a chance to really get to know who you are and to unleash what you want. It helps you realize that you really do have the power to have anything in your wildest dreams.

There are so many great aspects to the course. I just recommend you take it if you're struggling with anything in your life at all. This will knock it out of the park. Bye bye limiting beliefs. One of the exercises that I did was a board breaking exercise. I won't tell you all the details because I think it's something that you really need to do. I will tell you this: I broke the board and it felt great. I can't even begin to describe that overpowering feeling of getting rid of some of those limiting beliefs that I have been putting on myself for a long time. This course changed my life.

Sometimes people in my life will ask why I do so many self-help courses. I guess my question to them is, "Why don't you do them?" I mean, I've taken my business to a new level, and I've developed personally in ways I can't describe. It's all because of the self-help courses and viewing them as mentors.

This topic is near and dear to my heart, and I will never stop trying to grow and become a better person. The only person I need to be better than is myself. I never compare myself to anyone else, and I don't have any jealousy. Do I admire others? Of course I do; but I know that I can accomplish things that are amazing.

Having many mentors that you look up to will help keep you motivated and inspired, and believe me, you will need them along the way.

Take Care of You

This has been a tough one for me, and I feel as if many business owners struggle with this. Self-care is everything. You need to take care of yourself because, if you don't, who will?

I've always put my business at the top of my list of things to take care of, and sometimes it has hurt me in ways I can't explain. I was working super long hours and not living a balanced life. What's the point in that? It never lasted long; it was always just a moment in time.

When I first started the business, I didn't take much time for myself. It was nerve wracking knowing that I had to pay my bills and worry about whether I would have enough food or could pay my rent.

I didn't take much of a paycheck in the beginning of my career, so I was lucky to have my husband, who basically supported us in the beginning when we started this business. It was tough to find balance until I felt the pain that most business owners feel when they say they haven't taken a vacation in a long time. I totally get how you can be so immersed in your business that you just don't take any time for yourself. Now, if you start from the beginning taking that time for you, then you never have to change that habit, even if it's just one hour a day. Think about it. Use the morning hour or the evening hour to just carve out some time for yourself; you will be ahead of the game.

Catch 22, I've been great at this. I take a minimum of two vacations per year, and countless weekend trips. I never say I don't have time. I put it in my schedule so that no one can disturb this time that is much needed. This is part of growth; this is part of living a life of balance and being able to enjoy the fruits of your labor. If I can just give you one piece of advice, please stay balanced; please take care of yourself, or you will end up rundown, broken and burnt out, because you didn't take enough time for you.

This year was life changing for me. Believe it or not, even during the pandemic, I found a way to take my health to a new level by using the app called Noom. Have you heard of it? It changed my thinking about food. I changed my diet and lost 20 pounds. I started eating more fruits and vegetables, and I learned things in the seminar with Tony Robbins that I never knew before. I also started drinking more water, which is something that most people don't do. You should be drinking a minimum of eight glasses of water a day. If you're not doing that, change it immediately. You will notice a huge difference in your health just by improving water intake.

I also move my body. I don't know what that means to you, but for me, it means going for at least one hike a day with my dog Stuey, and when Sandy was around, with her as well. This has been my regimen for the last 20ish years. Nothing, and I mean nothing, will ever stop me from going for my hikes and long walks. When you put your health first, it's amazing what you can accomplish. Anthony decided to get a Peloton bike and membership for us when the gyms closed. Our bike arrived on December 17, 2020. It changed our life. He built a gym in our basement. It's my place of zen and our happy place.

I also enjoy going to the spa, getting manicures and pedicures, and getting my hair done. I enjoy regular massages and going to the chiropractor. All of these things make me really happy.

You will feel more energized; you'll be happier. You'll be able to give more to your clients, and you will live a more positive life. It's an all-around win-win.

Peer Groups

Throughout my life, even before I started my business, I've always had a great group of peers (friends) that were interested in what I was up to. Some of my best friends have been there through my whole life, and we remain friends to this day. My best friend Vicky (Woods) Ross and I have been friends since kindergarten. It's crazy when you think about how long you have been friends with someone. We do a lot together. I've watched her kids grow up, and she has the most amazing boys. I admire her and her husband, Andrew Ross, for being such great parents. We're close friends with their entire family; they are my family. Sue Woods, Sheila Woods and Mark Golding are also my besties for life.

I also remain friends with Amanda Von Besser, Karen Meeker and her husband Derek, Christine Giampietro and her husband Marco, and Kelly and her husband John. It's fun to know that when you haven't talked for quite some time, you can pick up the phone and call, and it's right where you left off from before.

A new peer group I developed over the pandemic was the group of groomers that I met who wanted to join me in a great cause called the Worldwide Pet Grooming Association. It was an association that I started because I and a bunch of groomers believed that grooming was an essential need of the pets. We were strong believers in this. There were many people in the industry that didn't believe in this cause. That's why I started the association. A bunch of people reached out, and we all fought the good fight. It was quite extraordinary to have a bunch of fellow groomers who felt the same way as myself. Believe it or not, I was one of those who did my best to try and stay open if possible during the pandemic so that we could serve our clients and their pets.

This peer group helped me stay focused on getting heard so that we could get grooming salons back open and take care of the pets. I could write an entire book on this subject, but if you want to hear more about it, I'd be more than happy to share. I can't thank all these groomers enough, because in a time where we were all struggling, we stuck together and thought of ways, through Zoom, that we could be heard for the pets. Even though there were groomers that didn't join the association, there were some that also believed the same thing, so the message was getting heard. We were one of the first industries to open back up. It was great to know that we could make a difference and remain open, even with all the restrictions.

I also must give a shout out to Monika. She and I worked together in a time where no one else would work. It was just her and me slugging it out, even though we were both terrified to work. So many people were telling us we couldn't or shouldn't, but we didn't believe that. She was literally there for me when no one else was, except for my husband. It's hard to talk about, but during the pandemic, a lot of crazy stuff happened, and I'm sure that the way people reacted was due to fear, and the hurt was very real. I'm not saying that I was perfect, but I was trying to get heard and no one would listen. I know that people are afraid during a pandemic; I get that. And I'm not going to get into the details about my thoughts. I'm not here to create any enemies; I have my opinion, and it's gotten me to where I am today.

Having peer groups that see eye to eye with you, in certain situations, makes you feel supported and understood, and you can stand together, hand in hand (just kidding, not during COVID-19, but you know what I mean), to accomplish something great.

Read Lots of Books

I read a lot of inspirational books. Reading helps give you the perspective of someone else and what they've gone through. You may pick up something from a book that you can implement in your life. I have learned so much through reading. As I mentioned previously, the book that changed my life is called The Secret. What The Secret is about is that whatever you send out into the Universe, you are going to get. For instance, when I bought my purple Jeep because I wanted to be branded with my business, I had hardly ever seen any purple Jeeps before. As soon as I started driving around in it, I would see purple Jeeps. If you have a negative thought, you will attract that negativity. If you have a positive thought, you will attract that. Another book that I love is called The Power of the Subconscious Mind by Joseph Murphy. It is kind of like The Secret; it just tells you about the message in a different way. I'm always looking for a good read, so if you have any suggestions of books that have changed your life, feel free to send me a message on Facebook and let me know what they are, please and thank you. You can find me on Facebook (Tanya E. Ierullo) or on Instagram (poochesnpals).

Another one of my favorite books, which is specifically for groomers, is called Notes From the Grooming Table. I use this book every day in the grooming salon as a cheat tool to make sure I can correctly groom the breed that comes in that day. I have some of the pages memorized, and I always recommend this book to new groomers; it's a must have.

Along with reading books, I suggest watching many videos. I can literally sit for hours and watch grooming videos; it's a great way to learn new techniques for your practice. As a groomer or as a business owner, the learning never stops. It's important to find new ways to make your clients happy and keep them engaged, as well as provide different services that can accommodate them. Find new things you can do with your clients and their pets.

Do you know how many hours it takes to become a master of something? Well, if you guessed ten thousand hours, you would in fact be correct. Malcolm Gladwell's book Outliers explains this and what it takes to master a skill. Ten thousand hours is approximately 416 days, which is 59 weeks, and that's approximately 1.13 years, to be exact. But to learn a new skill doesn't take that long; it technically only takes 20 hours to learn a new skill. When you start something new, give yourself the time and patience that you need to succeed. Once you've gone through all that time, you will then begin to realize that mastering that skill was something you really wanted to do. This is probably why most businesses fail within the first year: giving up too soon when something great is around the corner. You must be patient with yourself. I try to tell my students every day to not be too hard on themselves, and that they're going to make mistakes, but they're going to overcome them and get better.

Take Lots of Notes

Whenever I go to a seminar, or when I read books or learn from someone new, I take lots of notes. Many great leaders say it's easier to learn if you write it down, because it helps you process the information faster. I have numerous notebooks, and I also keep a journal; it's been on and off over the years, but I recently just started it up again. Some of my notes from my second book, Pet Grooming Is Like Mountain Climbing, which will be coming out later this year, came from my journal, the one that I used to write in about Africa, and also my journal from when I did the Inca Trail to Machu Picchu in Peru.

When you take notes, you have them for a later date so that you can review them once you have forgotten what you wrote down. You can also use this information later to teach others things that you've learned.

For the majority of my life, I've had what I call a vision board. I write down all of my goals for the year, and as I reach those goals, I check them off my vision board. Tony Robbins said, "If you don't write it down, you don't get it," and that is clear as day. This year, for instance, I wrote down my vision board goals, and I reached every single one of them within six months. I truly recommend starting one, and if you need any ideas, I'd be more than happy to help guide you through a vision board. I include, in my vision board, words and pictures of the goals I want to achieve.

Here is a little secret I will share with you: One of my

goals, I keep as my main password to all my emails, banking, etc., so that it reminds me of what I want to accomplish. Once I reach that goal, I will change it to my next goal. Sometimes I've had the same goals for quite some time, but it doesn't mean I failed; it means that I am taking longer to achieve that goal. It can be frustrating at times, but you just have to keep plugging away. For the longest time, I had a goal to visit Africa. I started dreaming of that goal when I was about 10 or 12 years old. The point is that it did take me a long time to achieve that goal. When I was 30, I went to Africa and climbed Mount Kilimanjaro.

In a nutshell, taking notes comes naturally, and it's done in many different forms. Whatever way works for you is great. I have also taken video footage of myself stating something that I want done, so that I can review it later. That way, I can feel the emotion I felt at the time, what's important and what I want to achieve.

Chapter 7

Staying Focused

Be Positive

Making sure you stay positive is important. Starting a new business is hard. There will be many obstacles along the way, but if you remain positive, it will be easier. It could be through daily affirmations, like saying to yourself in the morning as part of your routine, "I am beautiful; I am kind; I am generous; I am inspiring; I am giving; I am a creator of my own life; I am driven; I am spontaneous; I am sexy; I am thriving." You get the picture. (Imagine doing this for 30 days in a row. Do you think you would notice a difference in your attitude?) It could also be through continuous learning, pep talks with your hubby, calling a friend, asking for advice, exercising, or whatever works.

Sometimes it is hard to stay completely positive, especially when others are trying to bring you down (but are they really?). For instance, during the pandemic, I know that things were tough for everyone. I fought to stay open because I felt we were an essential business. Some of the strangest things happened. There were people calling bylaw on me, left, right, and center, to let them know I was open so that they could shut me down. I truly felt that we needed to be open for the animals. In cases like this, it is tough to stay positive.

There were people looming out front of our salon, taking photos of us while we were grooming dogs. There were also people on some Facebook groups saying we were open and clearly stating that we shouldn't be open. It was hard when everywhere I turned, it felt like people were trying to take our business down. Bylaw called several times to mention that we were not essential. It got to the point where they came to the salon and handed me a notice of contravention, which stated we had to close our doors. If we didn't comply, we would be fined up to $500,000. That day was terrifying for me, and I wanted to crawl under a rock. That was not a positive day.

I remember tearing up; I thought that that was the end of business for me. I couldn't think straight; I had blinders on. It wasn't until I got home and had a chance to think about it for a few days that I started to do something about it. I started doing my research and came up with everything I possibly could. I called our ward 1 councilor, Stephen Dasko, and asked for his help on this matter. I also called our MP, Rudy Cuzzetto, and our mayor, Bonnie Crombie. They did their best to try to figure out whether we were essential or not. They ended up fighting for us in a meeting amongst Council. Mississauga was the first area to open pet grooming again. So we were allowed to open our doors again, on May

18, 2020. It was one of the most grateful days of my life. Then a lot of the other cities started opening up as well.

Even though I triumphed, my heart was still breaking for the businesses that didn't make it through the pandemic. Businesses had it rough, and it makes me very sad that some did not make it through this terrible storm. In business, it's important to remember that with the positive things that happen, there is always the possibility of potential storms. You must have an open mind to be an entrepreneur. There will be good days, great days, and bad days.

The downsides of running a business can be exhausting at times. For example, when first starting out, there is a lot of worry about money and where it's going to come from to operate the business. When I first took over the business, I had an employee who worked with me, and she was a great groomer. Of course, it's always nerve-wracking taking over a business and having someone you don't know work for you. I'm sure it was nerve-wracking for her as well. We made it work for a year. We went from a one-person to a two-person salon very quickly. I remember trying to book just a couple of dogs for myself a day, and the phone would only ring one or two times a day. It was frustrating knowing how hard it was to book appointments.

All the clients were used to the previous groomer, and they didn't want me to groom their dog, which I completely understand; I had to gain their trust. I remember it being hard for me at first to work in the new space. I was a lot slower than the other groomer, but that was to be expected. I was getting used to a new space, new clients, and new systems. I do remember days of bliss, where I had to pinch myself in disbelief that I finally had my own salon. It really did come naturally to me to have my own business. I always had difficulty being told what to do by employers, so to be my own boss was incredibly rewarding.

Being an entrepreneur is not for everyone. I can't even tell you how many times in life I wanted to give up. Going through those emotions can be mentally draining. I'm happy I never did though. I had a strong support system; my husband Anthony and my family and friends always believed in me and made it easy for me to believe in myself. This made the bad days better. There were countless times where I cried myself to sleep. Not knowing is the hardest. The first few years in business are always the toughest. According to statistics published in 2019 by the Small Business Administration (SBA), about 20% of business startups fail in the first year. About half succumb to business failure within five years. By year 10, only about 33% survive. If you know this going into business, it will make the good days and bad days easier to understand. Knowing is half the battle. I just love this quote by Mae West: "When I'm good, I'm very good. But when I'm bad, I'm better." Another quote, by John D. Rockefeller, is: "Don't be afraid to give up the good to go for the great."

My technique for getting through the tougher days is to have positive quotes or sayings in every space that I look at, to remind me that things will be better. A saying that is near and dear to my heart nowadays is to "be grateful and calm." As a groomer, this is a very important philosophy to live by.

Wouldn't it be nice if every day was a great day? Well, that's not always the case, and it never will be. When you feel like the whole world is crashing down on you, just remember that it's a moment in time, and the next moment is just around the corner.

Taking Chances

Making sure you stay positive is important. Starting a new business is hard. There will be many obstacles along the way, but if you remain positive, it will be easier. It could be through daily affirmations, like saying to yourself in the morning, as part of your routine, "I am beautiful; I am kind; I am generous; I am inspiring; I am giving; I am a creator of my own life; I am driven; I am spontaneous; I am sexy; I am thriving." You get the picture. (Imagine doing this for 30 days in a row. Do you think you would notice a difference in your attitude?) It could also be through continuous learning, pep talks with your hubby, calling a friend, asking for advice, exercising, or whatever works.

Sometimes it is hard to stay completely positive, especially when others are trying to bring you down (but are they really?). For instance, during the pandemic, I know that things were tough for everyone. I fought to stay open because I felt we were an essential business. Some of the strangest things happened. There were people calling bylaw on me left, right and center to let them know I was open so that they could shut me down. I truly felt that we needed to be open for the animals. In cases like this, it is tough to stay positive.

There were people looming out front of our salon, taking photos of us while we were grooming dogs. There were also people on some Facebook groups saying we were open and clearly stating that we should not be open. It was hard when everywhere I turned, it felt like people were trying to take our business down. Bylaw called several times to mention that we were not essential. It got to the point where they came to the salon and handed me a notice of contravention, which stated we had to close our doors. If we did not comply, we would be fined up to $500,000. That day was terrifying for me, and I wanted to crawl under a rock. That was not a positive day.

I remember tearing up. I thought that that was the end of business for me. I could not think straight; I had blinders on. It was not until I got home and had a chance to think about it for a few days that I started to do something about it. I started doing my research and came up with everything I possibly could. I called our Ward 1 councilor, Stephen Dasko, and asked for his help on this matter. I also called our MP, Rudy Cuzzetto, and our mayor, Bonnie Crombie. They did their best to try to figure out whether we were essential or not. They ended up fighting for us in a meeting amongst Council. Mississauga was the first area to open pet grooming again. So, we were allowed to open our doors again on May 18, 2020. It was one of the most grateful days of my life. Then a lot of the other cities started opening up as well.

Even though I triumphed, my heart was still breaking for the businesses that did not make it through the pandemic. Businesses had it rough, and it makes me very sad that some did not make it through this terrible storm. In business, it is important to remember that with the positive things that happen, there is always the possibility of potential storms. You must have an open mind to be an entrepreneur. There will be good days, great days and bad days.

The downsides of running a business can be exhausting at times. For example, when first starting out, there is a lot of worry about money and where it is going to come from to operate the business. When I first took over the business, I had an employee who worked with me, and she was a great groomer. Of course, it is always nerve-wracking taking over a business and having someone you do not know work for you. I am sure it was nerve-wracking for her as well. We made it work for a year. We went from a one-person to a two-person salon very quickly. I remember trying to book just a couple of dogs for myself a day, and the phone would only ring one or two times a day. It was frustrating knowing how hard it was to book appointments.

All the clients were used to the previous groomer, and they did not want me to groom their dog, which I completely understand; I had to gain their trust. I remember it being hard for me at first to work in the new space. I was a lot slower than the other groomer, but that was to be expected. I was getting used to a new space, new clients and new systems. I do remember days of bliss, where I had to pinch myself in disbelief that I finally had my own salon. It really did come naturally to me to have my own business. I always had difficulty being told what to do by employers, so to be my own boss was incredibly rewarding.

Being an entrepreneur is not for everyone. I cannot even tell you how many times in life I wanted to give up. Going through those emotions can be mentally draining. I am happy I never did though. I had a strong support system; my husband Anthony and my family and friends always believed in me and made it easy for me to believe in myself. This made the bad days better. There were a countless number of times where I cried myself to sleep. Not knowing is the hardest. The first few years in business are always the toughest. According to statistics published in 2019 by the Small Business Administration (SBA), about 20 percent of business startups fail in the first year. About half succumb to business failure within five years. By year 10, only about 33 percent survive. If you know this going into business, it will make the good days and bad days easier to understand. Knowing is half the battle. I just love this quote by Mae West: "When I am good, I am very good. But when I am bad, I am better." Another quote, by John D. Rockefeller, is: "Do not be afraid to give up the good to go for the great."

My technique for getting through the tougher days is to have positive quotes or sayings in every space that I look at, to remind me that things will be better. A saying that is near and dear to my heart nowadays is to "be grateful and calm." As a groomer, this is a very important philosophy to live by.

Wouldn't it be nice if every day was a great day? Well, that is not always the case, and it never will be. When you feel like the whole world is crashing down on you, just remember that it is a moment in time, and the next moment is just around the corner.

Making sure you stay positive is important. Starting a new business is hard. There will be many obstacles along the way, but if you remain positive, it will be easier. It could be through daily affirmations, like saying to yourself in the morning as part of your routine, "I am beautiful; I am kind; I am generous; I am inspiring; I am giving; I am a creator of my own life; I am driven; I am spontaneous; I am sexy; I am thriving." You get the picture. (Imagine doing this for 30 days in a row. Do you think you would notice a difference in your attitude?) It could also be through continuous learning, pep talks with your hubby, calling a friend, asking for advice, exercising, or whatever works.

Sometimes it is hard to stay completely positive, especially when others are trying to bring you down (but are they really?). For instance, during the pandemic, I know that things were tough for everyone. I fought to stay open because I felt we were an essential business. Some of the strangest things happened. There were people calling bylaw on me left, right, and center, to let them know I was open so that they could shut me down. I truly felt that we needed to be open for the animals. In cases like this, it is tough to stay positive.

There were people looming out front of our salon, taking photos of us while we were grooming dogs. There were also people on some Facebook groups saying we were open and clearly stating that we shouldn't be open. It was hard when everywhere I turned, it felt like people were trying to take our business down. Bylaw called several times to mention that we were not essential. It got to the point where they came to the salon, and they handed me a notice of contravention, which stated we had to close our doors. If we didn't comply, we would be fined up to $500,000. That day was terrifying for me, and I wanted to crawl under a rock. That was not a positive day.

I remember tearing up. I thought that that was the end of business for me. I couldn't think straight; I had blinders on. It wasn't until I got home and had a chance to think about it for a few days that I started to do something about it. I started doing my research and came up with everything I possibly could. I called our ward 1 councilor, Stephen Dasko, and asked for his help on this matter. I also called our MP, Rudy Cuzzetto, and our mayor, Bonnie Crombie. They did their best to try to figure out whether we were essential or not. They ended up fighting for us in a meeting among Council. Mississauga was the first area to open pet grooming again. So we were allowed to open our doors again on May 18, 2020. It was one of the most grateful days of my life. Then a lot of the other cities started opening up as well.

Even though I triumphed, my heart was still breaking for the businesses that didn't make it through the pandemic. Businesses had it rough, and it makes me very sad that some did not make it through this terrible storm. In business, it's important to remember that with the positive things that happen, there is always the possibility of potential storms. You must have an open mind to be an entrepreneur. There will be good days, great days, and bad days.

The downsides of running a business can be exhausting at times. For example, when first starting out, there is a lot of worry about money and where it's going to come from to operate the business. When I first took over the business, I had an employee that worked with me, and she was a great groomer. Of course, it's always nerve-wracking taking over a business and having someone you don't know work for you. I'm sure it was nerve-wracking for her as well. We made it work for a year. We went from a one-person to a two-person salon very quickly. I remember trying to book just a couple of dogs for myself a day, and the phone would only ring one or two times a day. It was frustrating knowing how hard it was to book appointments.

All the clients were used to the previous groomer, and they didn't want me to groom their dog, which I completely understand; I had to gain their trust. I remember it being hard for me at first to work in the new space. I was a lot slower than the other groomer, but that was to be expected. I was getting used to a new space, new clients, and new systems. I do remember days of bliss where I had to pinch myself in disbelief that I finally had my own salon. It really did come naturally to me to have my own business. I always had difficulty being told what to do by employers, so to be my own boss was incredibly rewarding.

Being an entrepreneur is not for everyone. I can't even tell you how many times in life I wanted to give up. Going through those emotions can be mentally draining. I'm happy I never did though. I had a strong support system. My husband Anthony and my family and friends always believed in me and made it easy for me to believe in myself. This made the bad days better. There was a countless number of times where I cried myself to sleep. Not knowing is the hardest. The first few years in business are always the toughest. According to statistics published in 2019 by the Small Business Administration (SBA), about 20 percent of business startups fail in the first year. About half succumb to business failure within five years. By year 10, only about 33 percent survive. If you know this going into business, it will make the good days and bad days easier to understand. Knowing is half the battle. I just love this quote by Mae West: "When I'm good, I'm very good. But when I'm bad, I'm better." Another quote, by John D. Rockefeller, is: "Don't be afraid to give up the good to go for the great."

My technique for getting through the tougher days is to have positive quotes or sayings in every space that I look at, to remind me that things will be better. A saying that is near and dear to my heart nowadays is to "be grateful and calm." As a groomer, this is a very important philosophy to live by.

Wouldn't it be nice if every day was a great day? Well, that's not always the case, and it never will be. When you feel like the whole world is crashing down on you, just remember that it's a moment in time, and the next moment is just around the corner.

Chapter 8

Taking the Proper Steps

Be in Control of Your Thoughts

Making sure you stay positive is important. Starting a new business is hard. There will be many obstacles along the way, but if you remain positive, it will be easier. It could be through daily affirmations, like saying to yourself in the morning as part of your routine, "I am beautiful; I am kind; I am generous; I am inspiring; I am giving; I am a creator of my own life; I am driven; I am spontaneous; I am sexy; I am thriving." You get the picture. (Imagine doing this for 30 days in a row. Do you think you would notice a difference in your attitude?) It could also be through continuous learning, pep talks with your hubby, calling a friend, asking for advice, exercising, or whatever works.

Sometimes it is hard to stay completely positive, especially when others are trying to bring you down (but are they really?). For instance, during the pandemic, I know that things were tough for everyone. I fought to stay open because I felt we were an essential business. Some of the strangest things happened. There were people calling bylaw on me left, right and center, to let them know I was open so that they could shut me down. I truly felt that we needed to be open for the animals. In cases like this, it is tough to stay positive.

There were people looming out front of our salon, taking photos of us while we were grooming dogs. There were also people on some Facebook groups saying we were open and clearly stating that we shouldn't be open. It was hard when everywhere I turned, it felt like people were trying to take our business down. Bylaw called several times to mention that we were not essential. It got to the point where they came to the salon and they handed me a notice of contravention, which stated we had to close our doors. If we didn't comply, we would be fined up to $500,000. That day was terrifying for me, and I wanted to crawl under a rock. That was not a positive day.

I remember tearing up; I thought that was the end of business for me. I couldn't think straight; I had blinders on. It wasn't until I got home and had a chance to think about it for a few days that I started to do something about it. I started doing my research and came up with everything I possibly could. I called our ward 1 councilor, Stephen Dasko, and asked for his help on this matter. I also called our MP, Rudy Cuzzetto, and our mayor, Bonnie Crombie. They did their best to try to figure out whether we were essential or not. They ended up fighting for us in a meeting amongst Council. Mississauga was the first area to open pet grooming again. So we were allowed to open our doors again on May

18, 2020. It was one of the most grateful days of my life. Then a lot of the other cities started opening up as well.

Even though I triumphed, my heart was still breaking for the businesses that didn't make it through the pandemic. Businesses had it rough, and it makes me very sad that some did not make it through this terrible storm. In business, it's important to remember that with the positive things that happen, there is always the possibility of potential storms. You must have an open mind to be an entrepreneur. There will be good days, great days and bad days.

The downsides of running a business can be exhausting at times. For example, when first starting out, there is a lot of worry about money and where it's going to come from to operate the business. When I first took over the business, I had an employee that worked with me, and she was a great groomer. Of course, it's always nerve-wracking taking over a business and having someone you don't know work for you. I'm sure it was nerve-wracking for her as well. We made it work for a year. We went from a one-person to a two-person salon very quickly. I remember trying to book just a couple of dogs for myself a day, and the phone would only ring one or two times a day. It was frustrating knowing how hard it was to book appointments.

All the clients were used to the previous groomer, and they didn't want me to groom their dog, which I completely understand; I had to gain their trust. I remember it being hard for me at first to work in the new space. I was a lot slower than the other groomer, but that was to be expected. I was getting used to a new space, new clients and new systems. I do remember days of bliss, where I had to pinch myself in disbelief that I finally had my own salon. It really did come naturally to me to have my own business. I always had difficulty being told what to do by employers, so to be my own boss was incredibly rewarding.

Being an entrepreneur is not for everyone. I can't even tell you how many times in life I wanted to give up. Going through those emotions can be mentally draining. I'm happy I never did though. I had a strong support system; my husband Anthony and my family and friends always believed in me and made it easy for me to believe in myself. This made the bad days better. There were countless times where I cried myself to sleep. Not knowing is the hardest. The first few years in business are always the toughest. According to statistics published in 2019 by the Small Business Administration (SBA), about 20 percent of business startups fail in the first year. About half succumb to business failure within five years. By year 10, only about 33 percent survive. If you know this going into business, it will make the good days and bad days easier to understand. Knowing is half the battle. I just love this quote by Mae West: "When I'm good, I'm very good. But when I'm bad, I'm better." Another quote by John D. Rockefeller is: "Don't be afraid to give up the good to go for the great."

My technique for getting through the tougher days is to have positive quotes or sayings in every space that I look at, to remind me that things will be better. A saying that is near and dear to my heart nowadays is to "be grateful and calm." As a groomer, this is a very important philosophy to live by.

Wouldn't it be nice if every day was a great day? Well, that's not always the case, and it never will be. When you feel like the whole world is crashing down on you, just remember that it's a moment in time, and the next moment is just around the corner.

Knowing Your Target Market

Identifying a target market allows marketers to focus on the most likely person to purchase their product or service.

Obviously, when opening up a pet grooming business, you are looking for clients with pets. If you groom dogs, it would be clients with dogs only, but it could also be that you groom cats as well, and your potential customer has both pets.

So how you find your target market is by talking to friends and family. You may also go out and network with business owners and vet clinics to find your target audience.

Finances and Accounting

When I first took over the salon, I have to admit, even though I had somewhat of a business plan in place, I still didn't really understand the costs of running a business. There are so many things that you need to buy, and it made it fairly difficult in the beginning to keep the funds flowing. I think it's really important to understand how everything works, and how much you need before you decide that you are going to take on the adventure of owning a business.

Just doing a little bit of research here and there will help you a lot to understand everything you need. Of course, it won't always be perfect, and it's always going to be a learning process: knowing how much you need to pay yourself, how much you need to keep in your bank account to cover the costs of the business, how much you need for supplies, for training, for fun, for education, for self-development, etc.

Someone once gave me great advice; they told me that I should get an accountant the day I start my business. Let's be honest; most of us groomers know nothing about accounting. It's true, right? Do you want to spend your time worrying about numbers, or would you rather pay someone who has experience to do that, and groom a dog instead? There are certain roles in your business that are just better off done by someone else.

I'm so happy that I took on my accountant, and she has been my accountant for the last 9 years. I am so grateful for Peggie; she has definitely made my life so much easier. Numbers are just not my thing, nor have they ever been. I don't know about you, but I don't really have any interest in knowing the accounting portion of the business. Don't get me wrong; I do like to know how well the business is doing, but that's a little different. The average cost for an accountant could be between 1,000 and 5,000 dollars per year. It's always good to have a few quotes from different accountants and to find one you can trust. You definitely don't want to skimp on this cost because it is ultimately going to help your business in more ways than one.

My accountant also helps me with payroll, and if I ever have a question regarding employee rights or changes with the CRA (IRS), or whatever it is, she is always there to lend a helping hand. She's even able to help me through a tough decision that I have to make, and lends guidance when I need it. I'm really so grateful and honored that she has been by my side for so long. Having people that you can count on is key to running a business.

As for finances, I recommend reading a few books. Some of my favorites are The Wealthy Barber, Personal Finance for Dummies, Rich Dad Poor Dad, The Richest Man in Babylon, Think and Grow Rich, and The Automatic Millionaire. I'm sure that you can find or Google any financial book, and it will help you along the way. As a business owner, I truly believe that we should be educated in many different areas in life.

When I Met Anthony

We met on Plenty of Fish. Approximately 9 years ago, we started messaging each other on Plenty of Fish. He messaged me first. I was intrigued, and we continued conversation. At first, for a little while, we were only messaging on Plenty of Fish, and then we exchanged phone numbers and started texting one another once in a while. Then we had our first phone call.

After that, we scheduled our first date, and I'd say that this process took about a month. It had been a long time since I had been in a relationship, or dated for that matter; so needless to say, I was a little nervous. Our first date was at a Tim Horton's near where his girls danced. I remember the conversation like it was yesterday. He said that he could only meet up for a little bit. I was totally okay with that because I didn't know if I'd like him. So I pulled up in my red Hyundai Excel, and to my surprise, there he was. It was a nice day in April; I remember that the weather was spring like, sunny and warm, but we were still wearing our coats. He had gotten a coffee and was sitting on a picnic bench out front.

We talked, and everything went very well. We seemed to get along, and it was really nice getting to know him on that first day. I think we agreed that we would see each other again. We were both pretty busy at the time, so I don't believe that we booked our next date, but we definitely kept in contact. From that point on, there were many other dates.

Our relationship blossomed right away. I wanted to hang out with him; I wanted to be with him. It was such a pleasure getting to know him, and I had definitely not met anyone like Anthony before. He made me feel special, and he was a true gentleman. He did things like opening doors for me. I remember in the early days that he would give me cute gifts, like homemade CDs with love songs on them. How cute is that?

We would go places together and have so much fun. He would take me to meet all of his friends, and he had lots of friends. For me, this was difficult in the beginning, because I was always convinced that I was shy. I had these limiting beliefs about myself in the beginning of our relationship, but now I realize that they were just that, limiting beliefs. I loved meeting his friends, and it was so nice. Everyone seemed so cool, and they kept telling me what a great guy he was. I now know how genuine they were being when they said that to me.

Anthony is like no other man I have ever met in my whole life. Believe me when I tell you this, because it's the truth. He treats me like a queen. He does everything for me. Not once has he ever called me a name or made me feel bad about myself and who I am. He's literally the best thing that has ever happened to me. The reason I tell you this is because I feel like if I didn't find him, I'm not sure if I would have blossomed into the type of person that I am today. He helped me grow in more ways than one.

I am so grateful that my honey came into my life. He has done more for me than you can ever imagine. And it is at this point in my life that I realize just how lucky I am that I met him. Having a partner that cares so much, and that is there for you in every way possible, is also something so special, and it will help you to grow in your business, as you have someone who supports you no matter what. You will always have someone that you can turn to when you need advice, or someone's shoulder to cry on when you are just having a really hard time. Some people don't have this, and I'm truly grateful that I do. I truly don't think that I would have made it all these years without him.

Take Care of Your Health

When starting a business, it is pretty new and exciting, but it is also nerve-wracking. It is easy to get wrapped up in the needs of the business, always saying yes and never taking time for yourself. This has to be one of the major mistakes that I made in the first 2 to 5 years of the business. You should always remember that your health should come first. After all, if you don't have your health you really don't have anything.

What is important to you about your health? What do you eat? Do you get any exercise? Do you meditate? Do you regularly see the doctor? Do you see a chiropractor? I do not just mean your physical health but also your mental health.

I have been learning from Tony Robbins a lot recently. I have been doing his priming exercises daily, and they really help me to focus in on my goals and my achievements, and to be grateful for the things that I have already achieved and that I am going to achieve. Your mental health is number one, and then your physical health. This is just my belief, so you can have whatever belief you want. Feeding your mind is so important to staying healthy and thriving. Tony says that what you focus on, grows. It is most definitely true.

Spend time focusing on positivity and growth; it is amazing how emotionally excited you will feel when you focus on these things. Have you ever been in a situation that was bringing you down? How do you feel in those moments? But if you focus on something like listening to some good tunes over and over, then you will most likely feel amazing, and it will get into your body and you may want to dance. At least, that is what happens to me. I don't know about you.

Working on your mental health and your physical health needs to happen daily. You cannot put it on the back burner and save it until later. It is incredibly important so that you can have that time with your business and your clients, and you can be happy serving them, knowing that you have taken care of what you need to first: you. If you keep putting your own health aside, you are not going to be happy. You are going to be miserable. And you will not be successful. So please just do yourself a favor and put yourself first for a change. You will thank me later if you decide to do this. It took me years to realize it, but it is finally coming to me now.

Accept Constructive Criticism

I know you think you are the best at something, and that is great, and you should. I have always believed that I am the best groomer in Mississauga, but that does not mean that I do not continuously learn. I put myself out there to learn from others. I have many different mentors that I look up to and learn from, and I like to allow people to give me constructive criticism so that I can become a better business owner and leader for my teams.

This makes me excited, because I am always willing to learn and get better. Being open-minded is key. Something that I have learned throughout this last year is to not take anything too personally. I used to be pretty bad for that. I used to take constructive criticism a little too seriously when I was a lot younger, not so much for grooming but when I worked at other jobs. I have grown so much since then, and

I welcome constructive criticism on a regular basis. I feel as if we can learn something new every day.

Nowadays, I am teaching at Best in Show Dog Grooming, and it is a lot of fun, and I am learning so much from the students, it is unbelievable. It is funny how you teach but you also learn from them. This new chapter in my life is really opening up my eyes to a brand-new, fun journey. I get a chance to constructively criticize the students on a regular basis, and they are very coachable and adjust as needed. I recently watched a podcast, and one of the speakers in it had said to always act like a student and be the least successful person in the room. If you act this way, you are bound to learn something new.

When you walk around the world pretending you know everything, you are never going to learn.

I just got back from the spa. I took a day for myself, which is rare, but I am learning how important it really is, and it is a Friday. I just noticed some activists standing on the side of the road with their signs, which say to stop portraying lies, and something along the lines of "kiss my ass." It amazes me that someone would want to stand on the corner like that and spend so much time focusing on something so negative, when there is so much in the world that you could be positive about and change within yourself. Rather than being so closed-minded, you need to express your opinion about how you are unhappy with something that is going on in the world. What I felt like doing was yelling out the window,

"Why don't you focus on something within, or being a better person, and read something that is going to make you happy?" But instead, I ignored it and just kept these thoughts to myself. Because really, that is what they want to do. And that is okay.

My Dogs

Growing up, I had Willie, which I've already spoken about. Sandy, my pug, came into my life the Christmas of the year Willie had passed. She was given to me as a gift on Christmas Eve. My sister Tiffany gave her to me, and she had a big red bow. She came running into the house and jumped right in my lap. I think she knew right away that she was my dog. Back then, I was working for the Beer Store, and I had several days off, so I spent all of my time getting to know her. Sandy and I quickly became the best of friends. This pug was so connected to me; she was my princess. One of my nicknames for her was Sassy Girl. Anyone who knew her knew this to be true. She had a really great personality. She was with me through my entire PetSmart career. She came with me when I started my business, and she was pretty much there for everything hard that I went through in my life.

Sandy always knew how to make me feel happy. She and I would go for the longest walks together. Some might say that a pug doesn't like exercise. Not her; she was the complete opposite. We would go for sometimes 2 hours in the neighborhood. I feel like we both felt we were so lucky to have one another. Sandy would always come to work with me every day; all the clients knew her. She was such a special dog. I just lost her in March 2021. She left me at the ripe old age of 15, just shy of her 16th birthday. It was one of the hardest days. I think about her still to this day, and it brings a tear to my eye. I think of her pretty much every day. The joy she brought me was like no other. I miss her dearly.

Stuey, a Toy Poodle, came into our lives when Sandy was 7 years old. I wanted a poodle so that I could get good at grooming them. It turned out that a friend on Facebook said he was available for adoption, so I talked to Anthony. We decided we would go and check him out. At first, he was really shy, and he wouldn't really come near us, but after a few minutes in the room at the vet clinic, he started to warm up to us. He was super cute, and we decided that he would join our family. When he met Sandy, she didn't particularly like him. I think she thought that he was going to go away. But he was sticking around. And she learned to love him. They aren't besties or anything, but they get along just fine. Sometimes I even see them sleeping next to one another, which melts my heart. Both of these dogs have made my life way more enjoyable. I remember the day we got Stuey; it was actually April 1st. So when we brought him to meet the girls, Madison and Mariah, they thought at first that we were kidding and it was a joke. We said nope, he's ours. They loved him right away.

They love Sandy too.

Chapter 9

Success Stories

Becoming an Award-Winning Groomer

I remember my very first competition in dog grooming. I decided to enter a Rescue Rodeo, which took place in Toronto at the T.O. Grooming Show. I remember being super nervous; it was my first competition, and I had no idea what was about to happen. I remember being greeted by one of the groomers who was a volunteer at the show, and they kind of explained a little bit about what was going on. A Rescue Rodeo is when you enter a draw and there are a bunch of rescue dogs that need grooming, and they draw a number and then that decides which dog you will groom. I remember I got a spitz. He was super cute, and he was quite good for grooming. There was a grooming truck on site, where I would give him a bath and blow dry him, clip his nails, clean his ears, etc., etc. I would make sure he got a really good brush out. All the other competitors also had dogs that they were grooming, and when we were finished, we would be judged on our work. There were usually three places: first, second and third. I did not place; however, I met a new dog and made him feel great so that he could find his forever home. I really think that every groomer should get in the competition ring. It definitely takes you out of your comfort zone and helps you learn even further.

I have done several other competitions in my time; not as many as some of my groomer friends, but I am happy with the ones I have done. I remember my second-ever competition, and I had a Wire Fox Terrier. Her name was Ruby; she was one of my clients' dogs, and she was a sassy little thing. But she did well for grooming. I was still really nervous on this day, but I ended up doing very well, and I placed second in this competition. Anthony still has the video, and I remember seeing the shocked look on my face. Everyone laughed when they saw my expression.

I was genuinely surprised and most definitely excited. They said that I probably would have taken first if I had gotten the eyebrows and the size of the face correct. This was a great learning moment for me. Not only did I place, but I also got a critique on how to make that groom better, so that when I go into the salon and groom this type of dog, I can make it look better for the client that comes in. It really is a win-win. Plus, when you compete, you are in a show with a whole bunch of people from your industry, and you can connect with them. It is just so much fun because we have so much in common, and we can share so much about our stories and learn from each other. Some of the greatest bonds that I have with groomers have developed at these shows. They truly are remarkable.

I could go on and on about grooming competitions, but I will not bore you with the details, even though it is exciting for me. I have also won many awards within the community. One of the first ones that I was nominated for was the Mississauga Readers' Choice Award. It was an honor, and we did not expect it. Someone had delivered a package that stated I was nominated, and I was humbled as it was my second year in business. So we ended up getting the gold in the Mississauga Readers' Choice, and that was so special. I remember we went for breakfast to celebrate with the Mississauga Readers' Choice, and the whole team came and celebrated.

Another award that Pooches N' Pals usually gets nominated for is the "3 Best Rated Salons in Mississauga." This award is based on several different categories: business hours, business images, complete information, social media, videos, website standard, acknowledgements, current evaluation, exact services, legitimate ratings, pricing, reviews and accuracy. So I love this one, and we have been nominated for this one for the last four years.

We also recently received, in 2021, the Consumer's Choice Award. This particular award was given as an award for customer service excellence. The CCA provides local businesses with special recognition that is both powerful and meaningful. Because the award is based on a survey of consumers with honest opinions, across a wide demographic spectrum, the CCA represents a "Seal of Excellence" that shoppers can take trust and confidence in.

Winning awards, especially when you are a new business, is really gratifying. When you start up a new business, it is tough, so getting recognized by someone is a great way to feel good and celebrate.

Donate to Your Favorite Charities

We have done a lot of donating in our time to different charities, such as the Oakville Humane Society and the Compass Food Bank. We've also brought coats and winter gear to local shelters that are in desperate need during the colder weather. Giving back is something that we've always done. Everyone should give back.

We have also given back to senior clients in need when times are tough, and we have given breaks on grooming for dogs in need, so that they can look and feel their best. I've also donated to Sick Kids over the years and several other charities as well.

Our current charity that we are giving to is the Lyons Foundation of Canada Dog Guides, located in Oakville, Ontario. They provide dog guides to people in need. This charity is near and dear to my heart, and I truly believe that dogs help people who have different disabilities. I am also getting a passion for the Earth and for sustaining our Earth. I have been wanting to give back to the world by making people understand the importance of planting trees, composting and cutting down on fishing, so that we can get back some of the planet that we are losing.

Know What Your Clients Need and Want

Over the years, I feel like I have developed a really great relationship with all of my clients. Mine are a select few. Knowing the type of haircut that they wanted for their pooch was extremely important to me and to them, because it gave them trust that I knew what I was doing, and then I could provide the service time and time again to make sure their pet looks super cute all the time. And if for some reason I couldn't get the look that they desired for their pooch, we would put them on a schedule so that we could eventually get that look.

I feel, as a groomer, it's really important to develop these relationships, and it's particularly important for clients to also have a relationship with the groomer and not have to bob around from groomer to groomer, because you'll never be happy, and you won't ever get the haircut that you desire for your pooch. Not all clients are going to want the exact same haircut, obviously.

If you take this kind of care and you follow up regularly, put them on a schedule and set them up for regular appointments throughout the year, you will definitely have a thriving business, one where people will want to keep coming back time and time again. I always pre-booked my next appointment with a client, or at least tried to, so that they had first pick of the slot that they wanted.

When you know the pet really well, it typically makes the groom a lot easier, because you know where their lumps and bumps are. You groom the same pet regularly, and they are really comfortable with you. And it ends up making your job a lot easier when you get to know the client of the pooch. Making sure to take proper notes and having them logged in your POS system will help to avoid errors with the trim later on. If the client wants a different haircut, that's not a problem. I used to have clients that would ask for something different almost all the time, and that also made it fun and enjoyable and kept them happy.

Growth in the Community

We often attend many community events, participate in most of the festivals and support local businesses. We build rapport with other business owners in the area, and we work on building relationships with people and with associations as well. Anthony has helped out a lot with events, such as Paint the Town Red and the Bread and Honey Festival. We have also volunteered for Buskerfest in Port Credit. Before the COVID-19 pandemic, we also took part in many networking events that took place at the Crooked Cue.

We just love Mississauga; there are so many great fun things to do. We also attended Hazel McCallion's 99th birthday and her 100th celebration online. It's really fun getting to know people in the community and being able to help out and take part in the different events. We are so excited because we're actually going to be putting on our own event in the near future. Ask us about it; it's going to be so great.

We just love the community so much that back in August 2019, we were married during Buskerfest, and the ceremony took place at around 11 a.m. It was the perfect day; the weather was amazing, and the people that attended were great friends and family. We couldn't have asked for a better turnout. We have been involved in Port Credit events for the past nine years.

Become Branded

I feel like I've been working on my brand for 23 years. I developed my logo many years ago and had my neighbor, Steve, digitalize it for me. It's been my logo for many years, and the only thing that's changed recently is that I made it a darker purple, and I changed one of the animals in the paw. The logo is key to becoming branded. It's also the colors that you use in your day-to-day posts and pictures on social media, such as on Google My Business, Facebook, Instagram and any other social media platform you use. Being consistent in how you portray yourself will familiarize your clientele with your brand.

For instance, there is a brand that almost everyone knows, and I'll give you a little hint here: Which business has the big yellow arches as their logo?

Did you guess McDonald's? Well, McDonald's has a brand that I would say the majority of the world is very familiar with. Do you agree with this statement? Everywhere you go, at every McDonald's, it's the same logo. They have the same kind of menu, other than a few differences here and there, and if you go to any McDonald's in the world, you will most likely have the same experience in each one.

So, over the years, I have been working on my brand. Recently, we started another salon. I took over the business of one of my friends, and we now have Pooches N' the Bluffs, which is located in Scarborough. We use the same logo; it just says Pooches N' the Bluffs instead of Pooches N' Pals. And doing this has made the brand a little bit bigger.

I'll tell you a secret: We have a goal to become franchised. This is going to take quite a bit of effort on our part; however, we are now on our second location and are currently looking for our third. I took branding to a new level; I ended up buying myself a purple Jeep. When I went shopping, it was one of the only ones left at the dealership. At first, I wasn't sure of the seat color, but I completely fell in love with it after a while. The inside color of the seats is brown. I also bought a tire cover that has the word Jeep, with paw prints made out of the two es. It's super cute and everyone knows it's me.

If you search for Pooches N' Pals on Google, it's no surprise that you will see many, many purple and yellow photos, because those are the colors of the logo. So if you need help with branding, feel free to reach out. It's something that makes me happy to help with.

Chapter 10

Ask and Ye Shall Receive

10

If You Don't Ask, You Don't Get

There are many lessons here with this topic. I have learned in life that if you don't ask, you don't get.

So I have learned in life to continuously ask for the things that I need and want. I asked the Universe to hire teammates. I ask the Universe for things all the time. Not only do I ask the Universe, but I ask others in my life when I do something. I remember when I asked to work at PetSmart. That day was a life-changing day for me. I decided to leave the Beer Store and go to PetSmart and work there full time instead. The reason I did this was so that I could do what I love.

I remember when I made the decision. I had talked to many people about it. Everyone said for me to follow my gut. Everyone had an opinion, but it may not have been in my best interest. So I really had to go with what I felt. It has literally been a life-changing, life-altering decision, and I look back on it and think to myself how grateful I am that I chose to go on the path of passion instead of the path of settling. The Beer Store was a really great job, and I really enjoyed it as well. I met many friends there, and I'm still friends with them to this day. So it's definitely an experience that I am grateful for as well.

When I made the decision to leave the Beer Store, the union manager had asked to meet with me to discuss why I was leaving, because when you get a job there, most people don't leave. I had worked so hard to get that full-time job, so they asked why I was leaving and if they had done something wrong. I remember them asking me these questions, and all I could say was that I was doing it for my future. I was doing this because I believed that there was a bigger purpose for me. Please don't get me wrong. I don't think that there's anything wrong with working there at the Beer Store, because I did it for many years. I just needed to do something different for me.

I don't just ask people for things that I want. I will literally sit here and think and dream about things that I want, and it's weird how I'll get a phone call, or an email, or someone will just randomly message me out of the blue, and that thing that I was thinking about will magically appear. I'm not saying this because I'm some force of nature, or am I? I actually believe that I am. I have been living this life for quite some time, and my thoughts have brought me so many amazing opportunities, I cannot even explain to you how they happen or why. But I truly believe that when you believe something, or when you think something, it will come true, whether that be good or bad. For instance, the example of when you're running late, and you seem to hit every red light on the way to your destination. Do you think that's a coincidence? It's not. It's because your mind is set to your lateness, so every single thing and every light is going to work with the way you're thinking, and it's going to give you every red light because you're thinking negatively about being late.

I could probably sit here and list off a million of these weird experiences that happened to me. They literally happen daily, but I won't bore you with the details. I will just let you know that my mind is very powerful in getting what I want. And I believe that everyone's is. I can sit here and think about some of the people in my life who are extremely negative. And it seems like something always goes wrong in their lives. "What you focus on, grows." This quote by Tony Robbins is definitely one of those game changers. Think about this for a minute: What you focus on, grows. So let's say you're sitting there thinking about how awful you feel about something. Well, if you're going to sit there and keep thinking about that over and over again, do you think you're going to feel happy, or do you think you're going to feel sad or angry? Just test yourself right now. Do two tests. Focus on something that makes you really happy, like a cute dog. Think about petting that dog, and the dog jumping all over you and wagging its tail. It's really happy to see you. Then you run around and you play with the dog. How does this make you feel? I mean, if you're anything like me, it will make you feel pretty happy and excited.

Now think of a moment that makes you really sad or mad, like if someone said something to you that was just so awful, like you're not a good person. Think of their tone of voice and how they're saying something so negative to you, bringing you down by calling you names and making you feel like a piece of crap. How does this make you feel? I mean, you can change your mood in an instant.

This is what I mean by "if you don't ask, you don't get," or "if you do ask, you do get it." It can really go both ways, so use your mind in a powerful way and train it to do things that will make you get the things that you want in life. You can literally have any life you desire. All you have to do is put your mind to it, and ask the Universe and ask the people in your life to make it happen.

Vision Boards

So, if you don't have one of these, you are missing out on an opportunity that can change your life for the better. When you have these goals in front of you all the time, you look at them daily. I have mine in my kitchen, and I go in there several times a day. This year, in 2021, I made a vision board, and the majority of the things came true by the middle of the year. Some of the things that I had on my vision board were to buy our second property and to be fully staffed at our Mississauga location. We did that with ease, thanks to my trusty business partner. He helped keep the momentum going for the business. Those were just a couple of things that were on the vision board that came true.

I can't remember where I first learned about vision boards, but when I heard about it, I was like, what? I thought that was such a cool idea. And I have had one, not every year but recently, and I will have one every year until eternity. I definitely need a vision board in my life. It brings me joy because I just love checking off things that I have accomplished. It really makes me feel good.

What else can I mention about vision boards? Well, I think it's really important to make them fun and unique. I tend to add a lot of photos, and I add different words to describe what I want, in detail, so that the Universe better understands it. For instance, one day, I would love to buy my parents a home of their own. That's on my list of goals on my vision board, to accomplish by 2024. Its a few years away, but it's definitely something that I'd love to do. Another thing would be to spend four months of the year, during the winter season, somewhere warm like Costa Rica or Florida. I haven't yet put this goal on my vision board, so no wonder it hasn't come true, but I'm finally putting it there, and it looks like it may happen next year.

When you have a vision board, you tend to make daily habits that allow you to accomplish small pieces of your goals towards your end goal. Another thing that was on my list this year was to hire someone to help with social media, particularly Instagram, because I felt like I was spending a bit too much time on there, and it was taking away from some of the other things that I could be getting done for the business. So I hired someone and, within two weeks, it happened. This is going to free up so much time for me, which is really exciting because now I have the opportunity to finish this book, which is at the top of my vision board.

Here we are, at the end of 2021, and I've accomplished more things this year than I could ever imagine. However, 2022 is going to be even better. I can feel it, because I'm putting in the right practices to make it happen. The vision board is just one piece of the puzzle. So if you need help creating a lovely vision board for yourself, you can reach out to me anytime you want, and I'd be glad to help. Sometimes envisioning your future isn't as easy as you may think, because you may have limiting beliefs that it will not happen. Don't kid yourself; you can do anything you put your mind to.

Writing a Journal

When I was younger, I used to write in a journal every day, but I thought of it more like a diary. It would help me get through and understand the day, and learn from it and make sense of everything that was happening. I have approximately 10 or more journals from my past, which could be a book in itself, LOL. I recently started journaling again, and it's really nice. At the end of each day, I write maybe one page about what I did that day. I talk about different experiences that I had, and/or conversations that I had with people, and then I figure out ways that I could possibly have made my day better, or how it could have changed or anything.

Writing down your feelings is an awesome way to learn and to recap. Everyone should have a journal. Find the right space to write. I usually write in my journal every night before I go to sleep. It's nice to close your eyes and reflect on your day, and write down moments of significance. You can also ask yourself questions about things that you want to achieve, things you want to get better at, etc.

I try to keep my journal as a positive thing that I enjoy doing daily. Once a month, it would be good to pull your journal out and read it, and see things that you've overcome, moments that you were proud of, things that made you happy, things that made you sad and things that you are grateful for. That way, everything is at the top of your mind. Speaking of which, I think I'm going to go back and reread my journals from when I was younger. You never know; there could be an idea in there that you had, which could possibly come to fruition.

You can consider journaling as a type of self-reflection that I have experienced, where you reflect on your life. I just recently read a statistic that only 16% of people actually write in a journal. That's a really low number considering what journaling does and offers.

You can make journaling as fun and creative as you'd like. You can add stickers and use highlighters and different types of fonts and pens. Just make it your own and enjoy it. Some of the most successful people that I've ever met have journals.

For instance, I have journaled when on vacation. My journal took me back to places where I've been, such as Kilimanjaro, when I climbed that mountain, and to Machu Picchu, when I did the Inca Trail. I have thorough notes from those days. Stay tuned for my next book, *Pet Grooming Is like Mountain Climbing*. My next book will be released soon, and I came up with the idea for that book during my book writing session with Raymond Aaron.

So, you can see the importance of journaling; it is key to success in life. I always wanted to publish a book but couldn't wrap my head around it. This has been 7 years in the making, and in the last few months, it's actually been quite easy to get it done. But if I didn't journal, then I might not have had a lot of the information that is in the book, because I wouldn't have taken those notes; plus, I have to say that my memory isn't that great, so it's really good to go back and reflect on the things that I used to do. Can you see the benefit in journaling? Send me a PM on Instagram,@poochesnpals.

When to Say No

I know it can be hard sometimes to say no, but there will be moments in your life where you just need to say no in order to grow. There were many times in my life where I had to say no to something that was going to get in the way of my dreams, like going to that party. Or saying no to that drink. Or saying no to the peer pressure of some of the situations from when I was younger.

"You say no to protect your yeses."

– Robin Arzon

Robin Arzon is an instructor through Peloton, and she wrote a book about running. She said this quote several times during her classes. I just love it. Her inspiration is admirable.

Saying "no" doesn't mean it's a bad thing. It means that you are saying yes to something else that is important to you. You don't have to go to that event someone wants you to go to; it has to be something that you want to do. What is something that you feel like you would like to say no to? It sometimes takes practice to say no.

Day Planners

I always had a small pocket calendar that I used to carry around with me everywhere. Then when cell phones got popular, I stopped doing that. I used to always use a planner of some sort. I found it was a great way to organize my days and plan for everything necessary. Then, when I was grooming full time, I had a giant appointment book, which allowed me to schedule appointments, and I would carry this thing with me everywhere. Needless to say, it was a little inconvenient and very bulky. But that is the way we did things in the beginning.

As for my personal life, the planning sort of stopped, because I didn't really think I needed it, other than a planner to plan events, like my wedding. I have always had some sort of a system for events that I have planned in the past. I write down all of my ideas, and then I check off when I have gotten these things done. I found that this always worked perfectly for me. So just recently, my business coach mentioned the RPM system by Tony Robbins. Now I am using it to plan out my life. There are three types of planners.

I have a success journal, a life planner, and a vision planner. I am literally just learning how to use them now. It takes a lot of effort to learn, but I know that once I have learned it, it is going to be amazing. The three-tiered system is going to literally change my life. I am super excited, and I think that everyone should have a planner. Well, at least the go-getters.

I am loving the vision planner because this one is more for larger projects, and I am going to do some pretty cool events this year that involve dogs, so stay tuned for that. We are going to need lots of help, and we are going to have a lot of fun doing it. So if you are interested in participating in any of the events that I am putting on, feel free to reach out anytime.

The life planner is great because it is for your day-to-day stuff. Since I am not grooming full time and I am working consistently on the business, I really need to plan my days hour by hour, day by day, week by week, and month by month. Each life planner is three months long.

Again, I am still learning how to use this properly.

These planners allow you to set your goals high, then take the small steps in order to achieve these goals. When you break it down like this, it makes it seem so much more achievable. It is literally the best thing since sliced bread.

Do you have any ideas that you would like to share with me about how you plan your days? I am always up for new ideas, and I welcome them. Another fun thing about these planners is that they come with fun stickers and fun words that make it much more interesting.

Who Do You Ask?

So when I say "who do you ask," I mean, for example, let us say you work for someone, and there is something you want, who do you ask? For instance, if there is something that you need and would like in order to make sure your work is easier to do, for example a dryer for grooming, do you ask the salon owner for it? Or do you just complain that you do not have it? If there was something that I needed to ask for, like more hours if I was working at a place and was not getting enough hours, I would ask the manager or person in charge. I would literally offer to take anyone's shift, and I would connect with the people that work there and let them know that if they did not want to work, then I would be happy to.

When to Ask

Well, I guess that really just depends on when it is the right moment, and that is something that you have to feel out to make sure the moment is right to ask whatever question you want. Sometimes the wind can determine whether your answer will be a yes or a no. I remember the day that I applied at PetSmart for a full-time position. I wanted to make sure that the salon manager was in, so when I got there, I asked when she would be in. And apparently, it was going to be within the next thirtyish minutes. So I felt like it was a great time for me to hang around and wait, so that I could speak with her about the possibility of working at that salon. Lo and behold, I waited, and it was the perfect time. She said, "Okay, let us schedule a working interview." She looked in her appointment book and scheduled it right away. So when is key sometimes. It might not be perfectly convenient for you, but if it is perfectly convenient for the other person, and it is something that you want, you had better make sure that you are available to make it happen.

How to Ask

All I can really say is to just do it. Like seriously, just ask the question. If it's something you really want, and you want it bad enough, then just ask, what the heck is the worst thing that's going to happen? They will either say no or they will say yes. If they say no, then you can just ask the next person, whoever that may be. If they say yes, then are you surprised? Excited? Maybe you're just in awe of the fact that you got something that you wanted.

Why Do You Ask?

I don't know the reason why you would ask, but I do know the reason why I asked for things: I've wanted a job, I've wanted to hire someone for a job, I've asked the Universe for something that I really wanted. Whatever the reason, if you don't ask, you don't get. I try to coach a lot of my friends and family on the purchasing of a home, for instance. A lot of people, for some reason, are afraid or don't know the process for buying a home, but it is actually really easy to do. All you do is find a real estate agent, and stick with that real estate agent, they will coach you through the entire process of how to buy a home. Now let's say you are scared to purchase the home because then you see it as a commitment that you're going to be locked into for quite some period of time. Well, you could be scared for the rest of your life, and that definitely won't get you to your goals. The worst thing that's going to happen is that you make the purchase and then you lose the home because you can't afford it. That is the absolute worst-case scenario. To be honest, I'd rather take the risk and go for it, than to always wonder what could have happened. You will spend years wondering. That's not a life I want to live. I'm a risk-taker. And I hope you are too. And asking for what you want in life is one of the greatest gifts. You will have so much joy if you just ask.

About the Author

My name is Tanya Ellis. I have been grooming dogs for the past 23 years. I remember when I first learned to groom, way back in the day, at my first job. And it stuck with me as something that I really love to do. Grooming dogs is my passion. I was in and out of jobs my whole life, bobbing around and not knowing where I fit in. It wasn't until years later that I realized how much I really loved grooming.

I started working for other people. I quickly realized that I wanted to work for myself one day. After years of working for others, including a few large corporations, I decided to venture out on my own. I took over a business that was already operating. From that moment on, I fell in love with being an entrepreneur. I thought that I might fail at it in the beginning. But that never happened. It has been a roller coaster ride, with many ups and downs and loop de loops. I truly believe that my husband has made a huge difference in how I view myself, as well as my determination to get things done. He has supported me through this whole journey and has made it much easier.

Pooches N' Pals is where I blossomed as an entrepreneur. I have learned so much about others and myself. Pooches N' Pals has won several awards: Mississauga Readers' Choice, Consumer's Choice, and the "3 Best Rated Salons in Mississauga," which we have regularly gotten for 5 years in a row. As an individual, I have placed and become an award-winning groomer in several grooming competitions in Ontario. I have also competed internationally. I am certified through CPPS (Canadian Professional Pet Stylist Association) in all Canadian Kennel Club groups.

Currently, I am the head instructor at Best in Show Dog Grooming School, where we teach animal lovers to learn the trade of dog grooming. I am highly involved in the community and give back whenever I have a chance. My favorite charity is The Lions Foundation of Canada Dog Guides. I truly believe they make a difference in people's lives.

www.ingramcontent.com/pod-product-compliance
Lightning Source LLC
Chambersburg PA
CBHW051157120626
46547CB00012B/1099